Seeds and Storms

Seeds and Storms

Royal

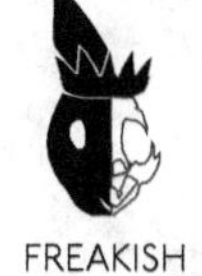

Freakish Publishing
Syracuse, New York

ISBN: 979-8-218-21736-5

Illustrations and cover design by Royal

For
anyone
who relates
to these words

Content warning: Suicide mention, self harm mention, body issues, grief, disconnection, de-realization, disturbing imagery

I've always been a conflicted person
Torn by my own thoughts
I have never been so set
Felt so certain
On anything
Until the thought came to me
Write a book

Table of Contents

Blinded in Heavy Rain

Blinded in Heavy Rain

When I yell,
Does no air come out?

Constant rain
It rattles my brain
Is friendship supposed
To bare this heart ache and pain?

It doesn’t feel real
But I can’t let go

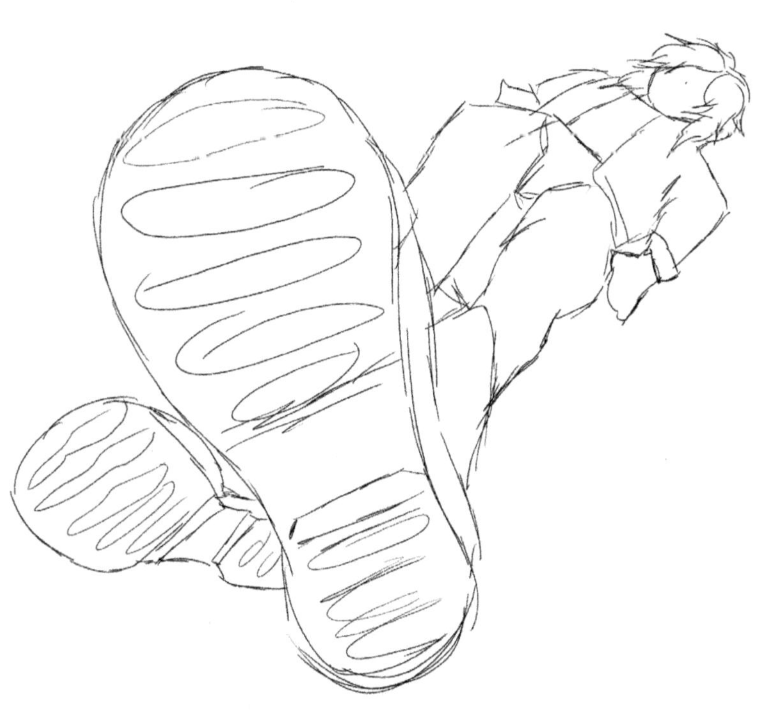

Did you hear me cry that night?
Were there tears in your eyes?
Don't forget me
In your new life

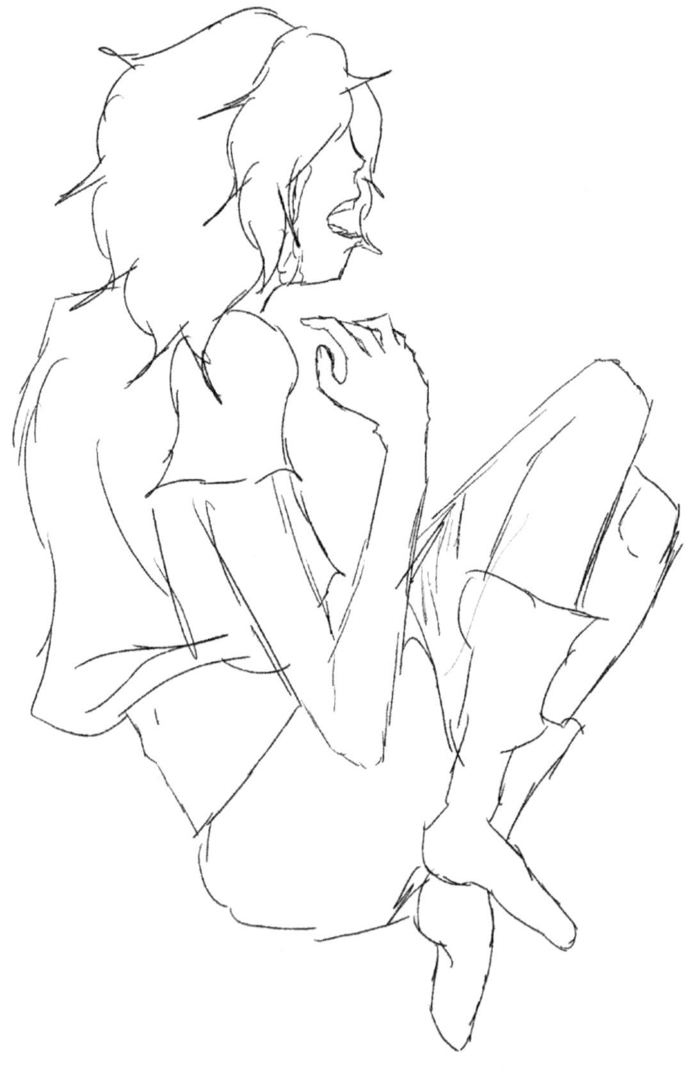

This isn't me
Not how I'm supposed to be
Please
Remember me the way I wrote myself out to be
When I still had only dreams
With no strings tied
The strings we call reality

I've spent life times
Searching
Wandering
Looking
For the one
Where I can thrive

Strong but weak
Certain but uneasy
A king but a peasant
Dead but alive
Decaying but beautifully
Someone who can’t make up their mind

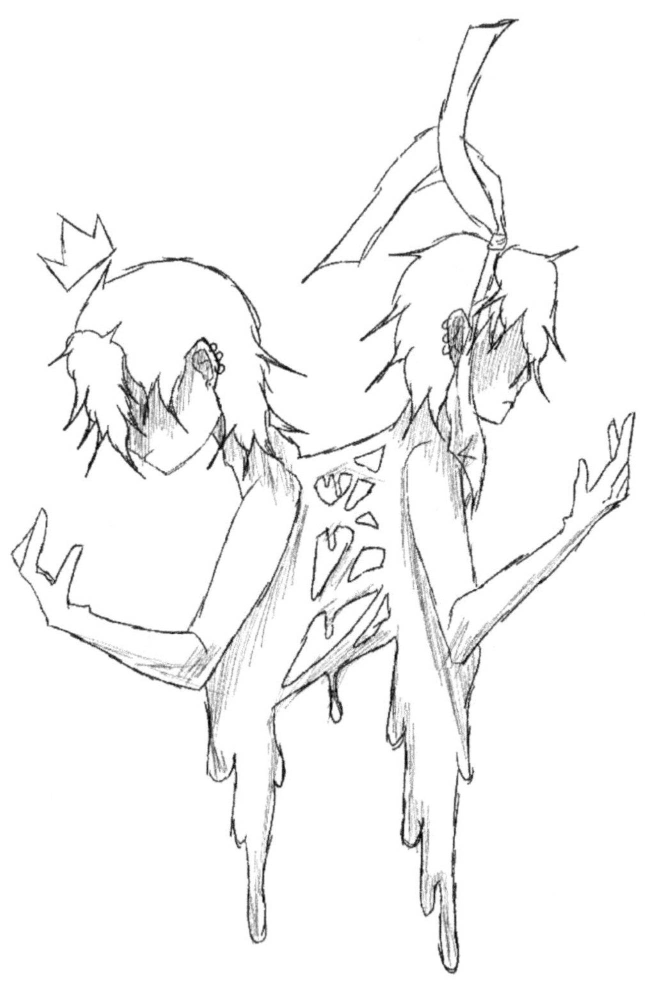

I'm not just having a bad day
My mind doesn't want me alive

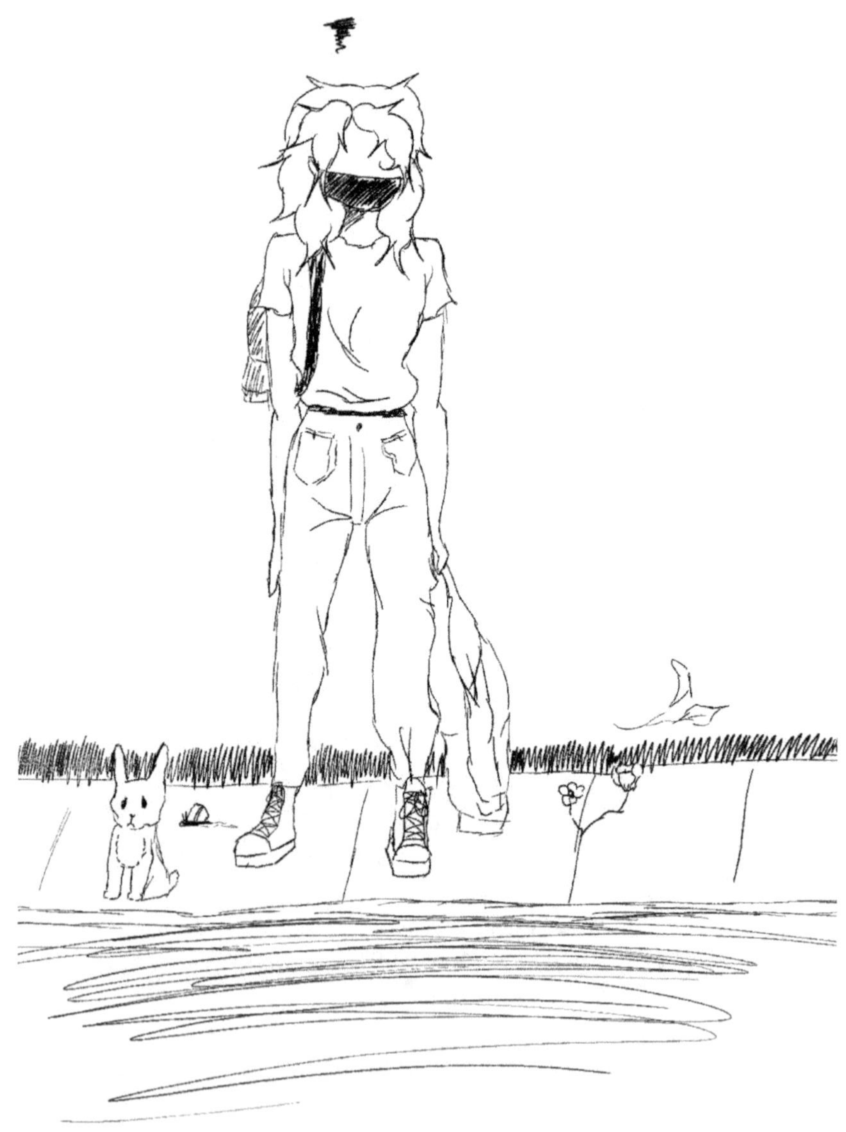

This body isn't mine
But I still take the pain
To pay rent

How can I miss memories
I've never made?

I'm sorry I'm always changing
I don't know how to see myself

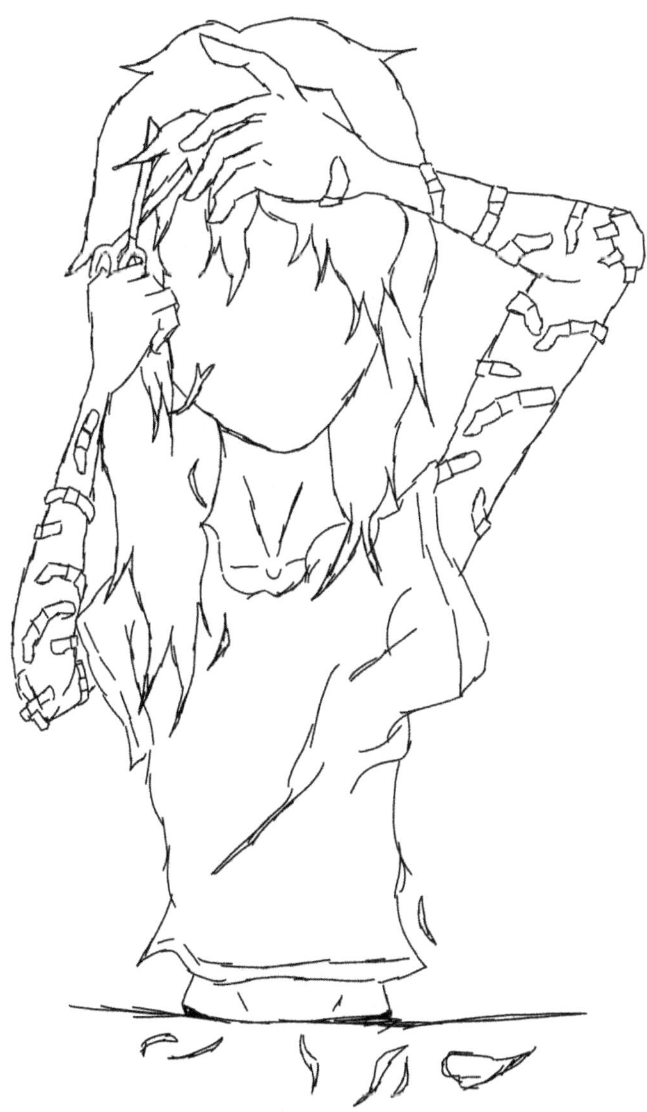

I'm not here
In my mind
Reality creeping
Ready to vanish

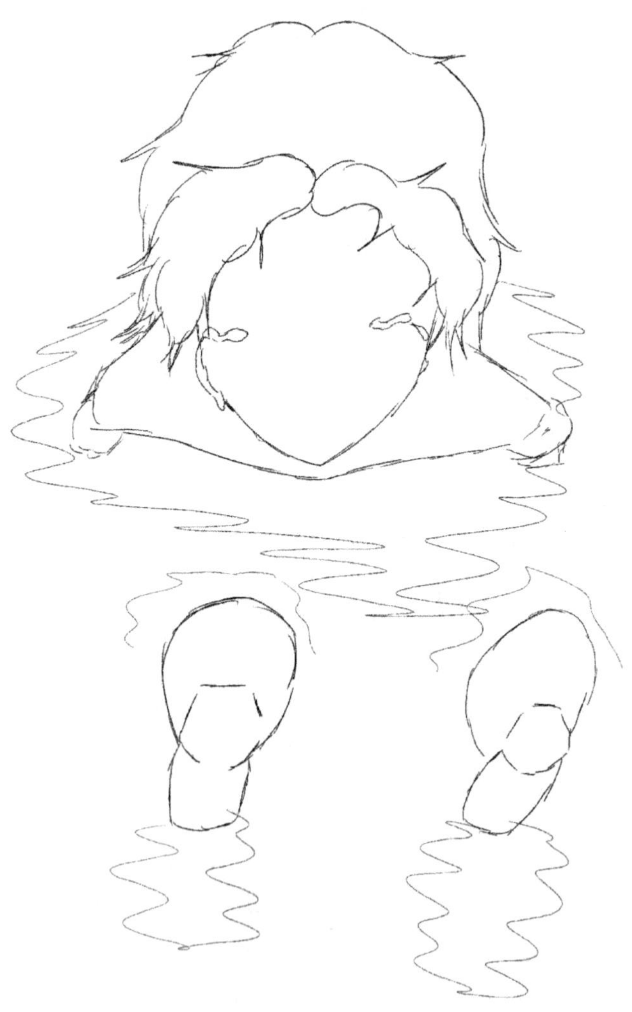

Never me, want to be
Connected to reality
But I'm not ready

Kinda want to break my arm
Possibly punch the wall
Make my knuckles bleed
Strangle myself so I can't breathe
Fall so hard my skull explodes
No that's not good
Don't let them know
Reset it's okay
Just make it another day
Shoot reminders in your veins
That physical pain
Won't make the mental stay away

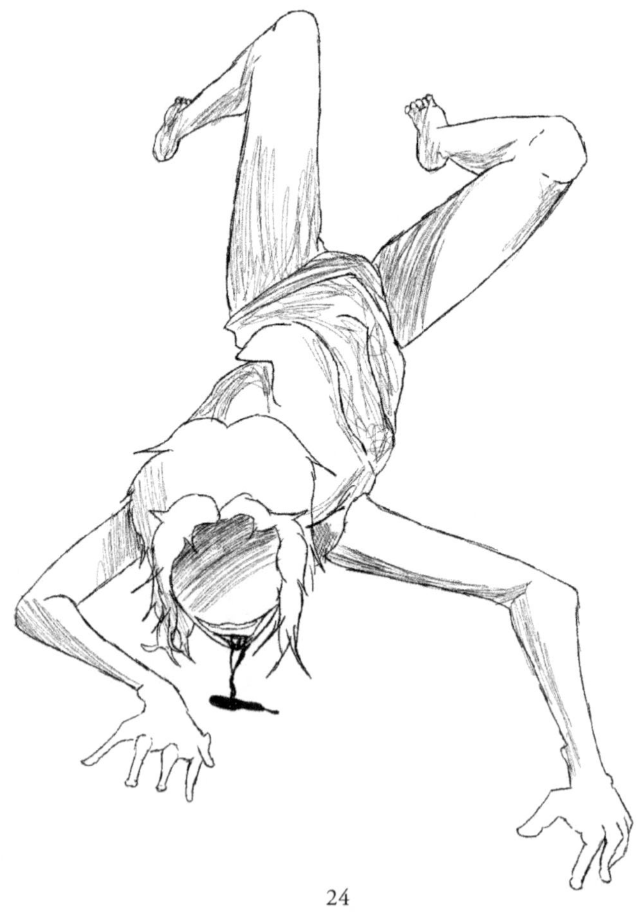

My soul has been screaming out forever
"Shut up!"
"They'll never hear a sound"
My brain blurts out

I bleed out trails of red
For every word I never said
Never to be healed or followed
Just wanted to let out the sourness of sorrow

I'm free falling
Trying to control where I land
I know I'll only break my legs

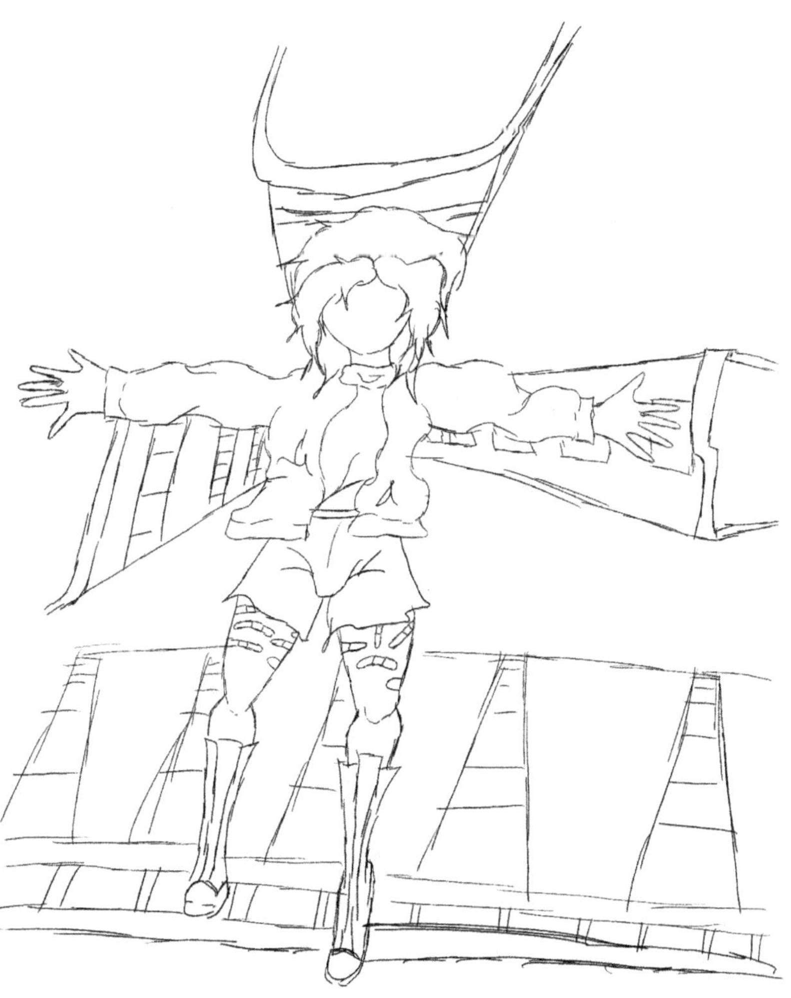

Can't you see the truth I am hiding
Everything around me is dying
Rotten and decaying
My mood keeps swaying
Just keep lying and denying
You're not losing your mind
Just complaining too much
Stop undermining others pain so much
-How could I possibly understand, right?

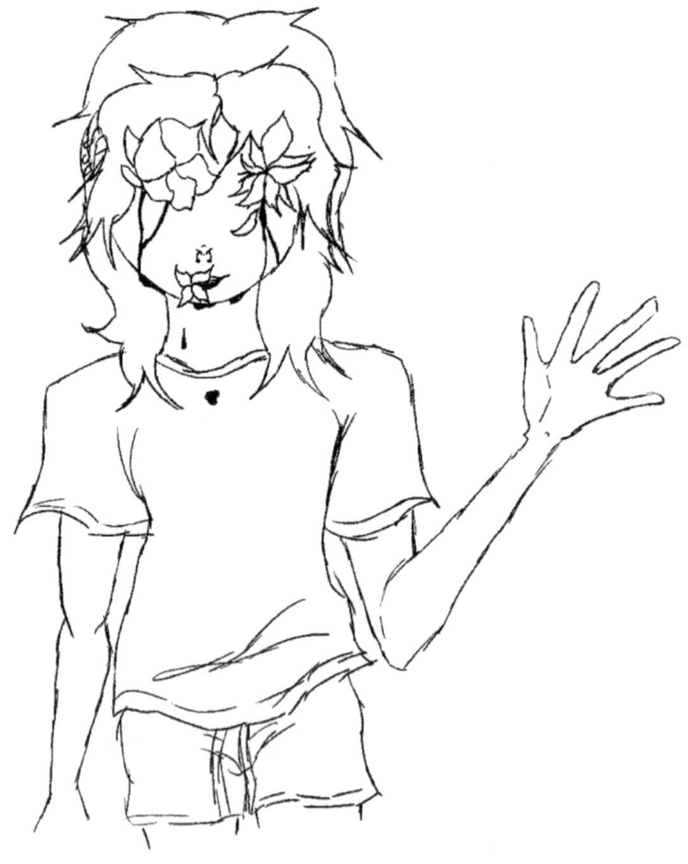

You're perfectly rare in every way
Even when you make a mistake
You know exactly what to say
But I am far from your equal
The only thing remotely beautiful about me
Is the way I decay
My ability to bend without breaking
Unlike you I am impossible to mend

Disrespect
It is the one thing I can't stand
But I am forced to deal with
I don't expect to have my needs met
Rather live in solitude
Than deal with your attitude
Tell me what have I done to be
Disrespected, reprimanded, and neglected
Why am I so emotionally affected?
I take in every moment for more than it seems
I show nothing, I'm disconnected
You say you respect me when in all honesty
You pity me, You mock and pick and poke
Unaware of how I've broke
I don't have the heart to tell you
But when I finally gain the courage to
I am to blame
For igniting your flame

Why am I always the one who ends up teary eyed
Saying the apology
That was meant to be mine

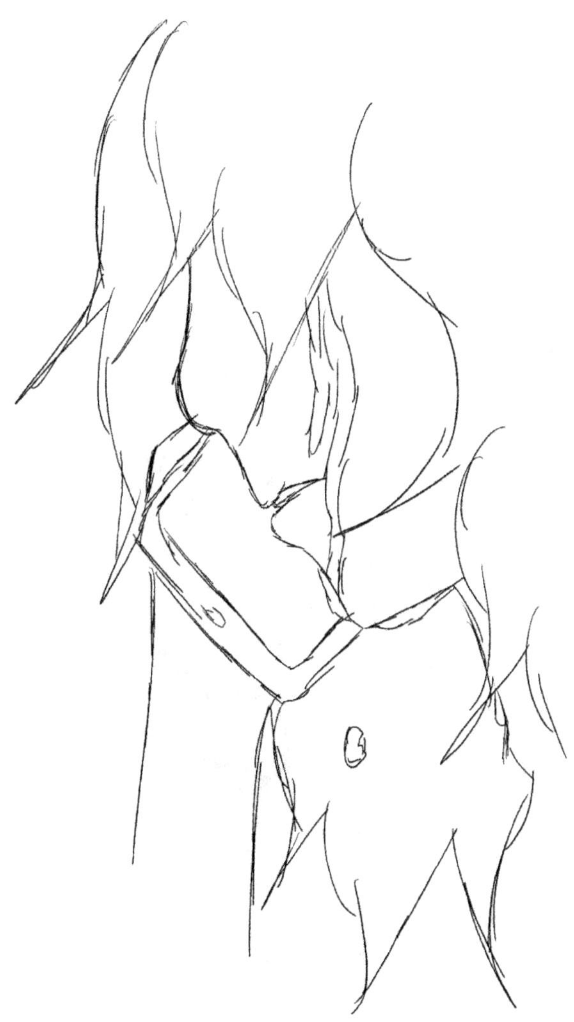

I think I'm going insane
I can't stop irrational ideas
From forming in my brain

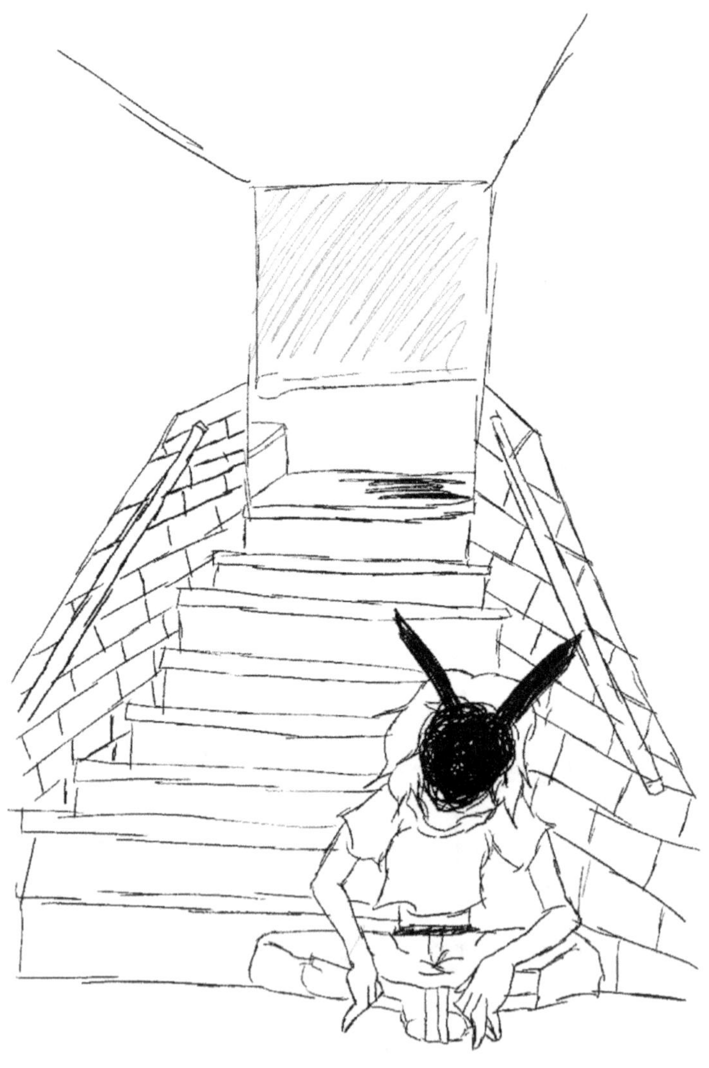

I'm sorry I am constantly in the state of change
I can't stand myself

I love the thrill of something toxic
It reminds me of you
You made me sick of myself
My stomach will feel weak
I remember one time
We were joking
I brought up Grandpa's tattoo
How he felt foolish because of the truth
You told me I tattooed myself too
You smiled and laughed
I was hurt and confused
Why would you smile
At the scars that wrapped my thighs

-My mothers words, about my self harm

I decided to be a nice person
I've been suffering the consequences ever since

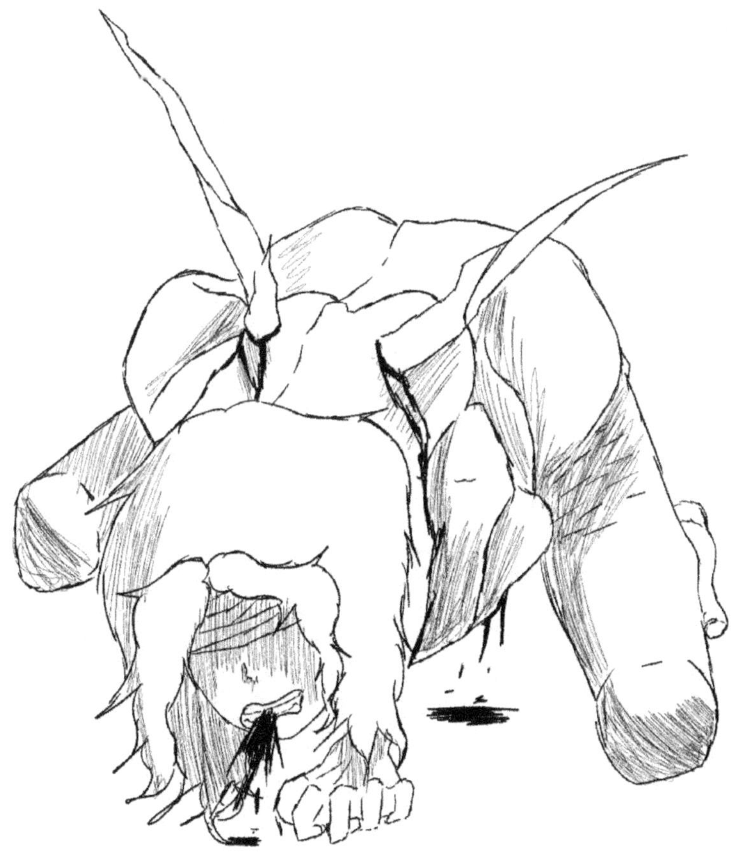

What if I looked like
What's on my mind?

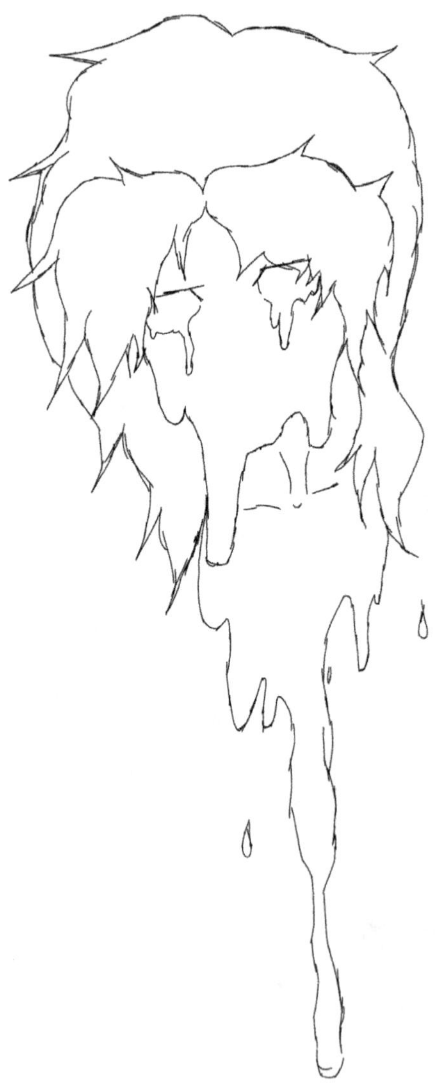

I just want to feel at home again
I'm getting way too alone again
Hoping to make it so I can feed my soul again

Times watching me
Pressuring me
To make my life happen quickly

Happy personality
Depressed soul
Impressive mind

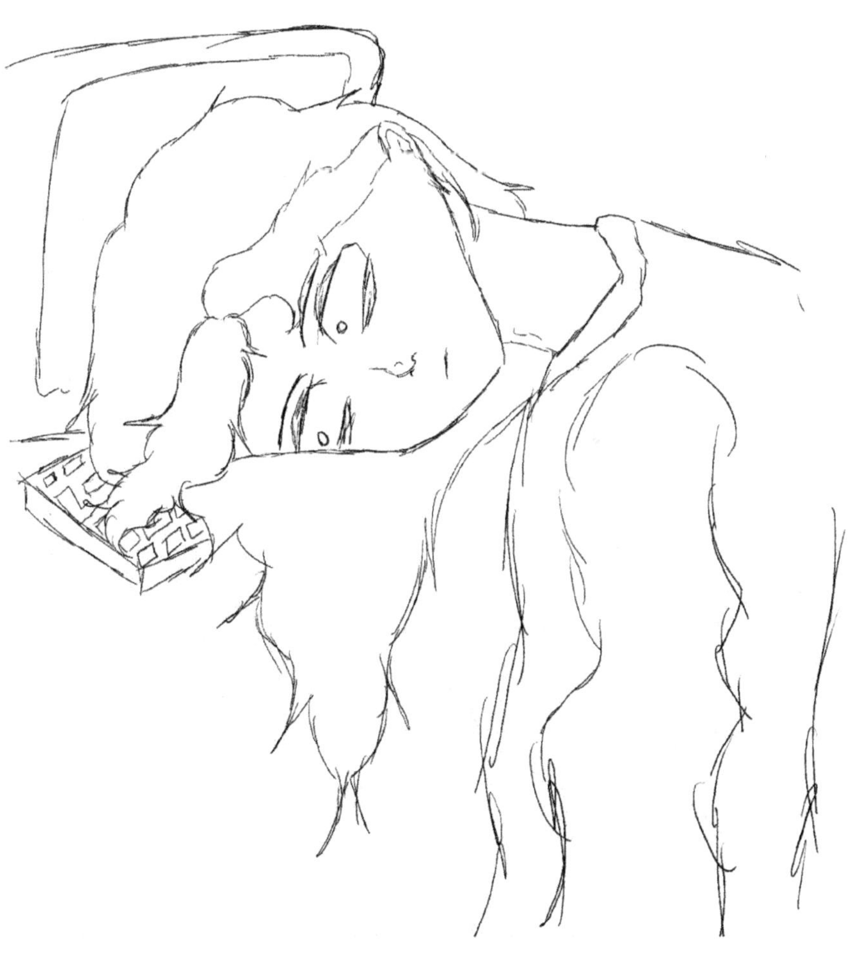

Break me
Take me to a place
To think about what it was like
To breathe clearly
And love myself the way I loved the world around me
"Endlessly"

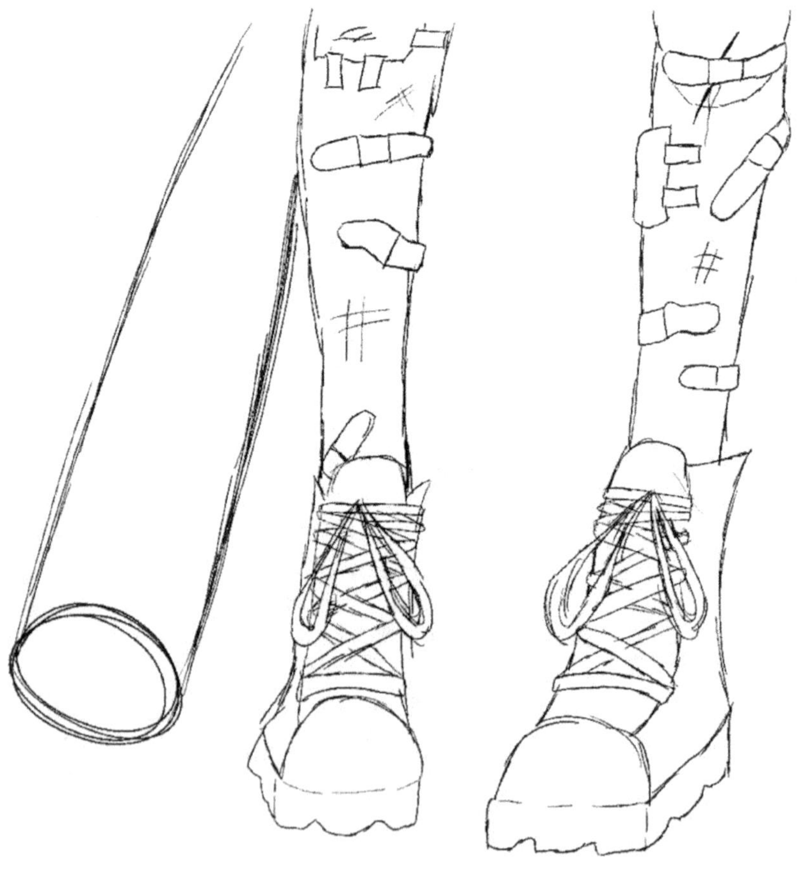

Can't remember half of my accomplishments
Can recall all the skills I lack
Don't feel worthy of all I hold
Even though I'm told I've worked so hard
Bending my back breaking and about to snap
Hanging by my feet or neck
Impostor syndrome always makes me reflect
It's my mind I'm trying to dissect

If I'm going to feel lonely
At least leave me alone

I strive for perfection
Fueling myself with the idea
Shoot reminders in my veins that it isn't real
But I'm so addicted to the pain of pretending
I'll drink this beautiful poison
I don't mind if it's slowly killing me
It's why we're alive, isn't it?

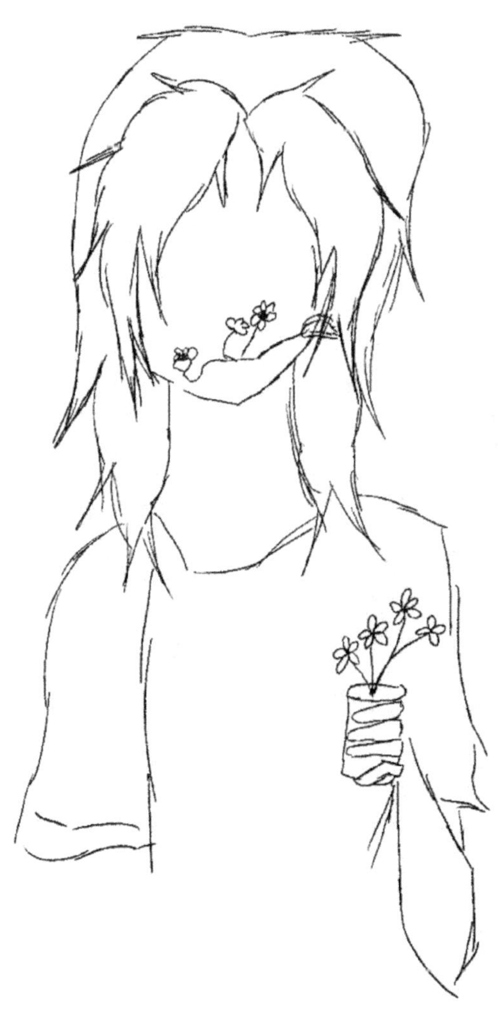

I can bend but not break
I already made that vial mistake
My poison spilled out on the floor
I stitched myself together
And pushed myself to spill more

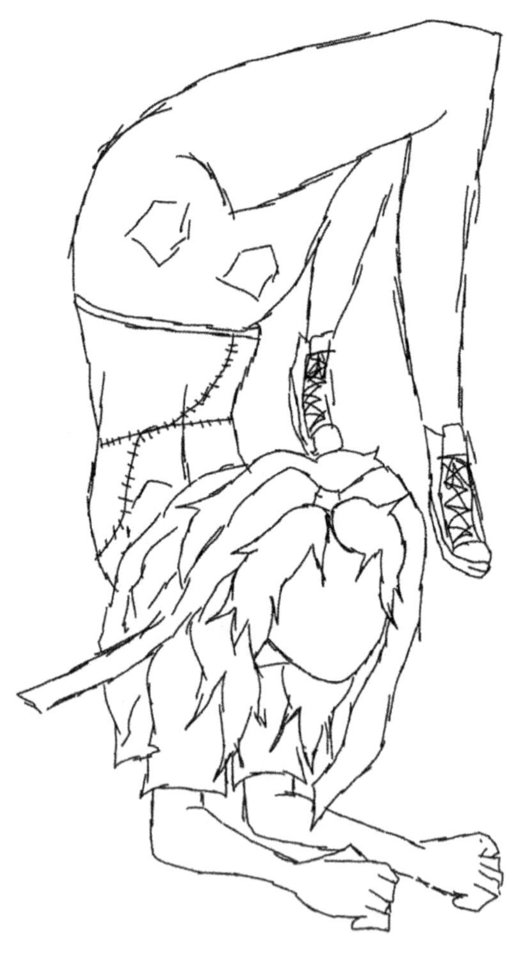

Forgive me
This isn't how I'm supposed to be
This isn't the me you were meant to see
But the fake version can't breathe
You drowned them and expected them to breathe

I'm stuck in a summer haze
My mind drifts for days
It's too fast and too slow
It doesn't feel the same
Everything just repeats itself
I can't tell if I'm just lacking room to grow
Maybe I'm finally too alone
Trying to learn to let go
I can't release
Then I'm face to face with the beast
No longer able to deny what is and isn't a fantasy
This can't be my destiny
I don't want my peace

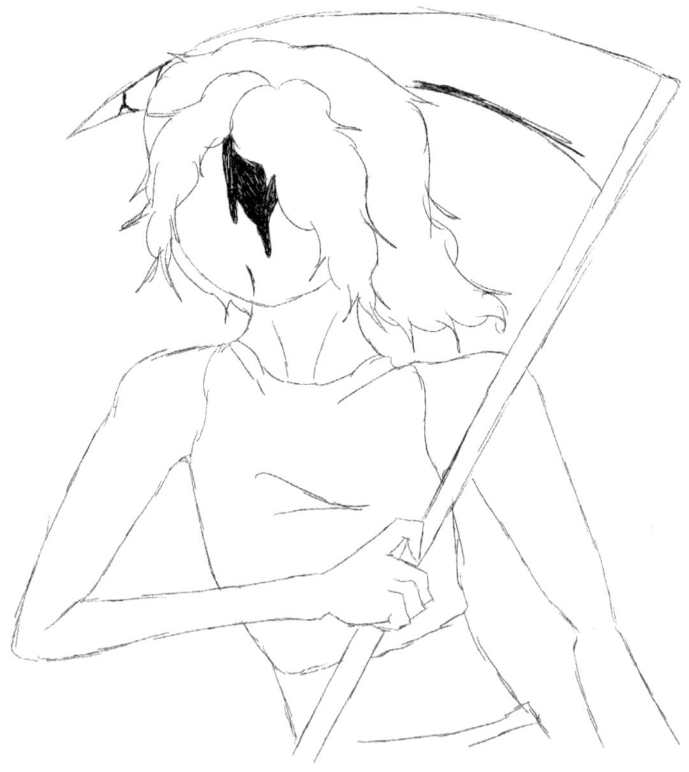

Born to a world of blood and violence
Chaos is always on my mind
Forced to lie
Hurry up and decide
Choose a side
Bleed out and hide
Don't be yourself
Don't bottle it inside
Argue for your life
Why am I the bad guy?

If there really is a greater power than us
Then fuck them
Fuck their system
It is the most gruesome thing
I have ever been a part of
They've hurt me in more ways I thought possible
Stripped me of worth and pride
And for what?
Their eternity of judgment
Of nothing

"Mature"
I've always been told
I exceed people's expectations in maturity
I knew how to adult
Better than most the adults around me
Some said an overachiever
Too much of a believer
That my childhood was lost to traumas
Thats been questioned and repulsed
Always my fault
I had to learn who I am
Before I could try and learn how to be me

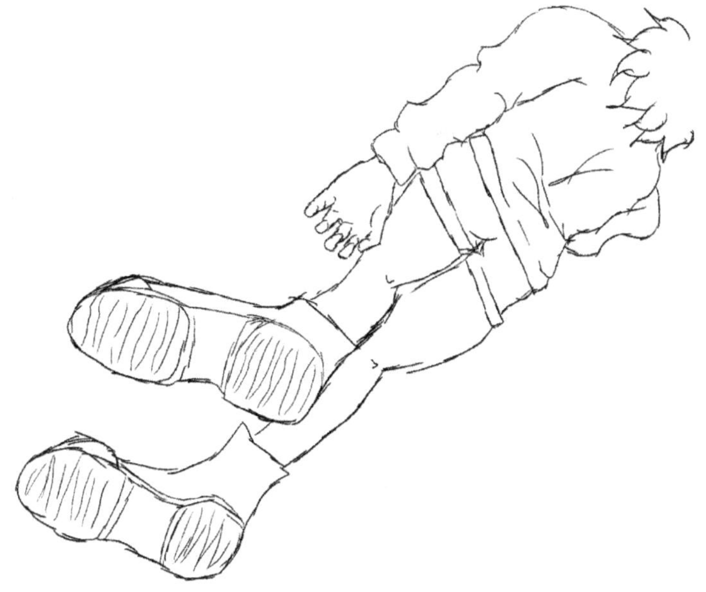

Somehow the pain that is displayed
Is better
More believable
Than what's in my brain

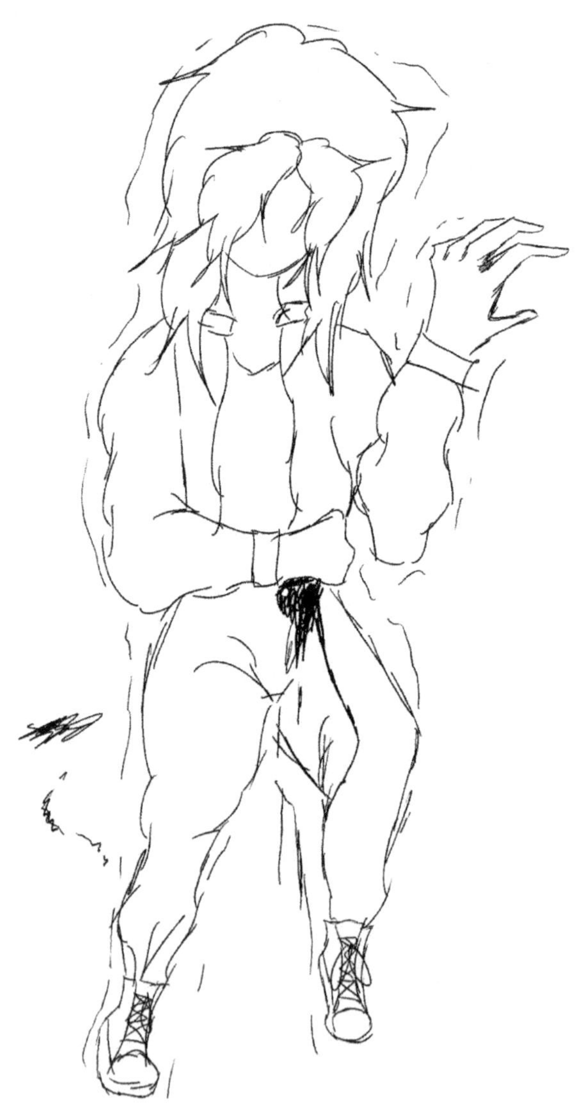

At what point in time did my
Love, spirit, and sex
Get used against me?
I thought my body was my only tortuous feature
Lost that thought to a preacher
Why can't my life be mine
It doesn't harm yours
My blood may be the same as yours
But my mind is so much more open
Than your closed doors

I’ve never known the feeling of something stable
I always had a million homes
Never learned to settle
Always to disappear
Now the world around me has vanished
Maybe my existence has simply evaporated
But don’t you fear
My thoughts weren’t always fatal

I cough out every bit of poison that fills my lungs
Back onto who it belongs too
Holding it in my gut, until it's time to cut
But now my chest is swollen
My mouth too use to the taste of the toxin
I've been inhaling all this bad air
Every venomous thought part of your plot
I've been devouring my own tongue
So you can have your fun
I've endured too much to act fine
To be alright
Now there's a sickness inside
I resign.

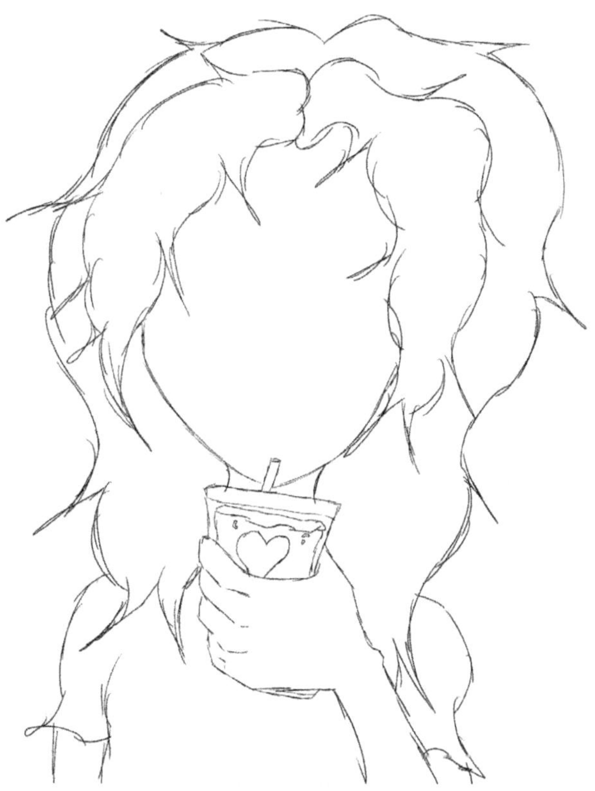

This air is suffocating
But the atmosphere is clear
The scars are pretty
But the wounds are ugly

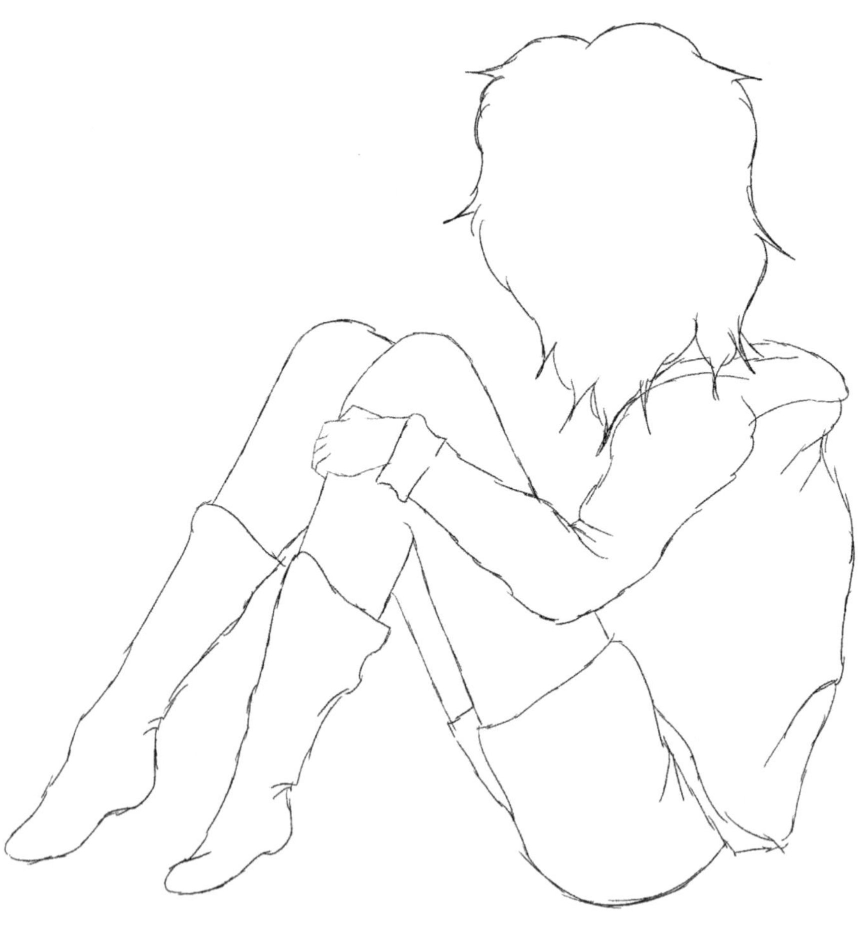

I died again tonight
Six months
It's been my longest life time
-Half a Year

I have everlasting wounds
My doctor said it's trauma
That word always leaves people confused
Claimed I'm too young
As if age determined anything in life
My body is young, but my soul wishes to be done

The sound of your voice
Pierced through every sound
I enjoyed
It dripped out of my eyes and mouth
The danger in your ways
Painted my reality
The colors
Stained my name

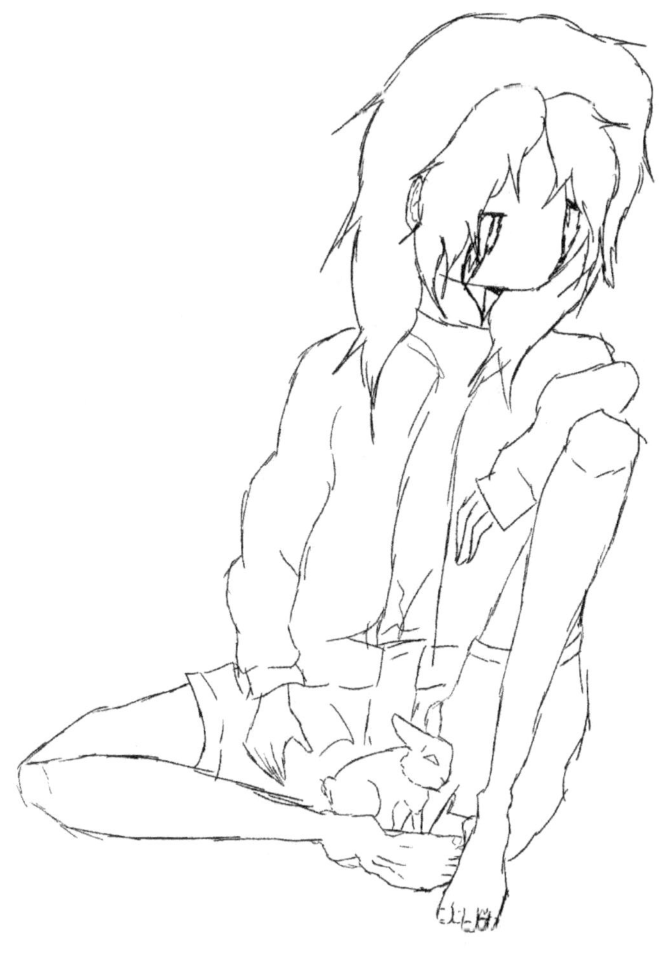

Battle everything internally
I'll be tired for an eternity
Doesn't feel right to say I'm fine
This isn't the way things are meant to be

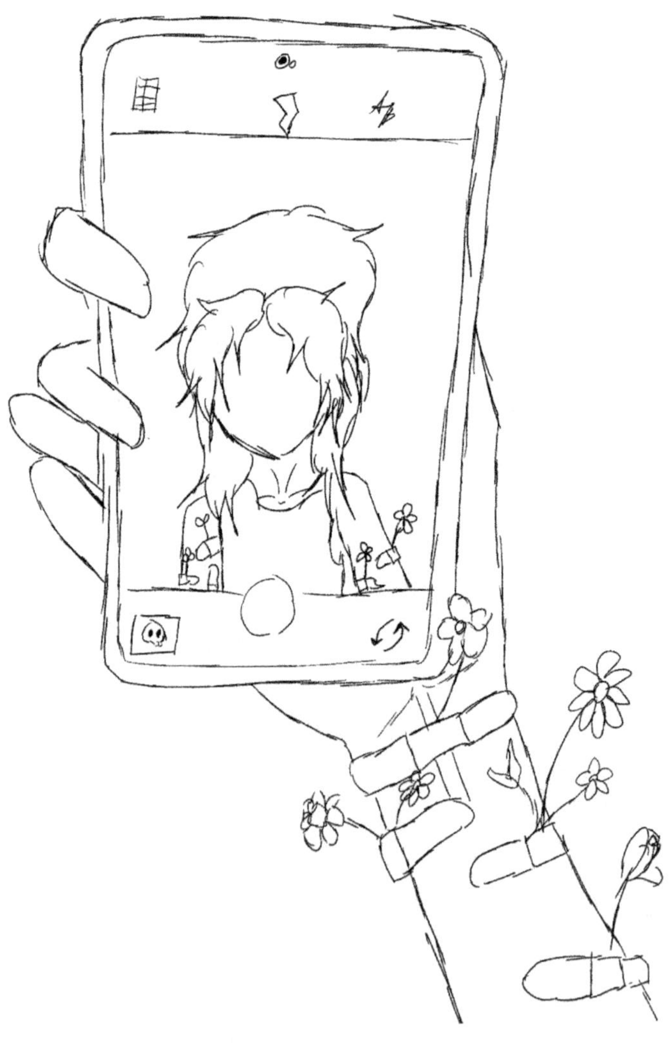

I'm sick
But not in a way you can see
Some other infectious disease
That slowly eats me alive
You don't realize
You're watching me slowly die

Someday when my mouth no longer tastes of metal
I will regret baring my teeth in my tongue
Biting it off and going numb

Same cycle everyday
Staying the same
Again again again
Makes me want to lift my legs and float away
When every line is the exact same thing
But worded a different way

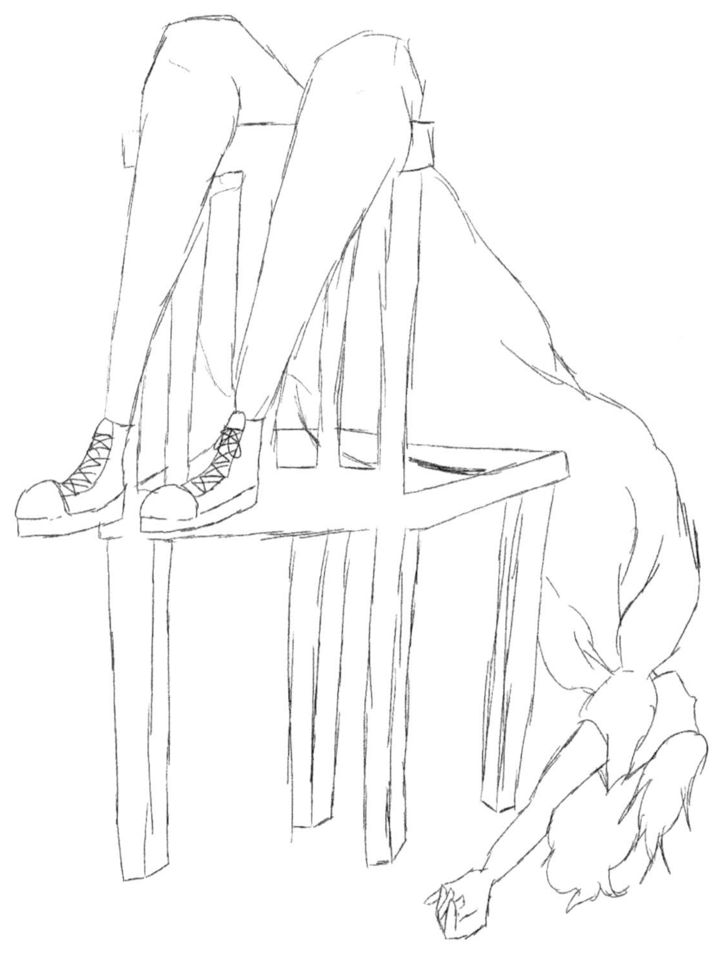

Just keep smiling
No one wants to know discomfort
Why would you tell them
When you're to blame
For turning out this way

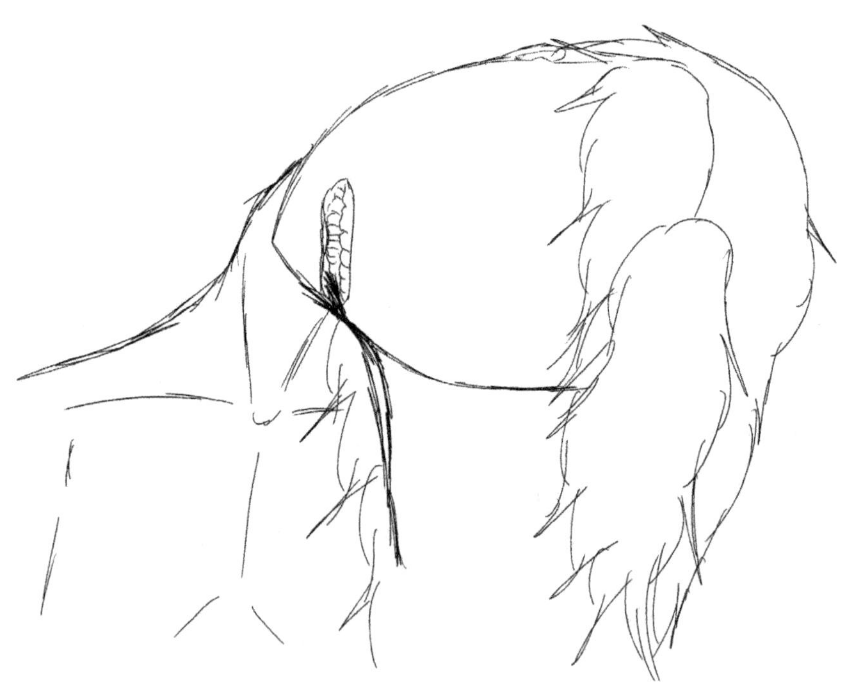

Take me apart
I'm all yours
Made for your desire
Adding to the fire
Too much has gone too far
You don't pick up the signs of my depart
You always had to be right when we would fight
But nothing was ever fine

You stole something from me
My peace
Every part of me that wanted to love
Please keep it
I don’t want to feel what you did again

I stopped asking how you were
I never stopped caring
You didn't care enough
You never showed it
It wasn't tough love
It was non-existent
You don't miss me
You miss how I treated you
I don't hate you
I hate what you did

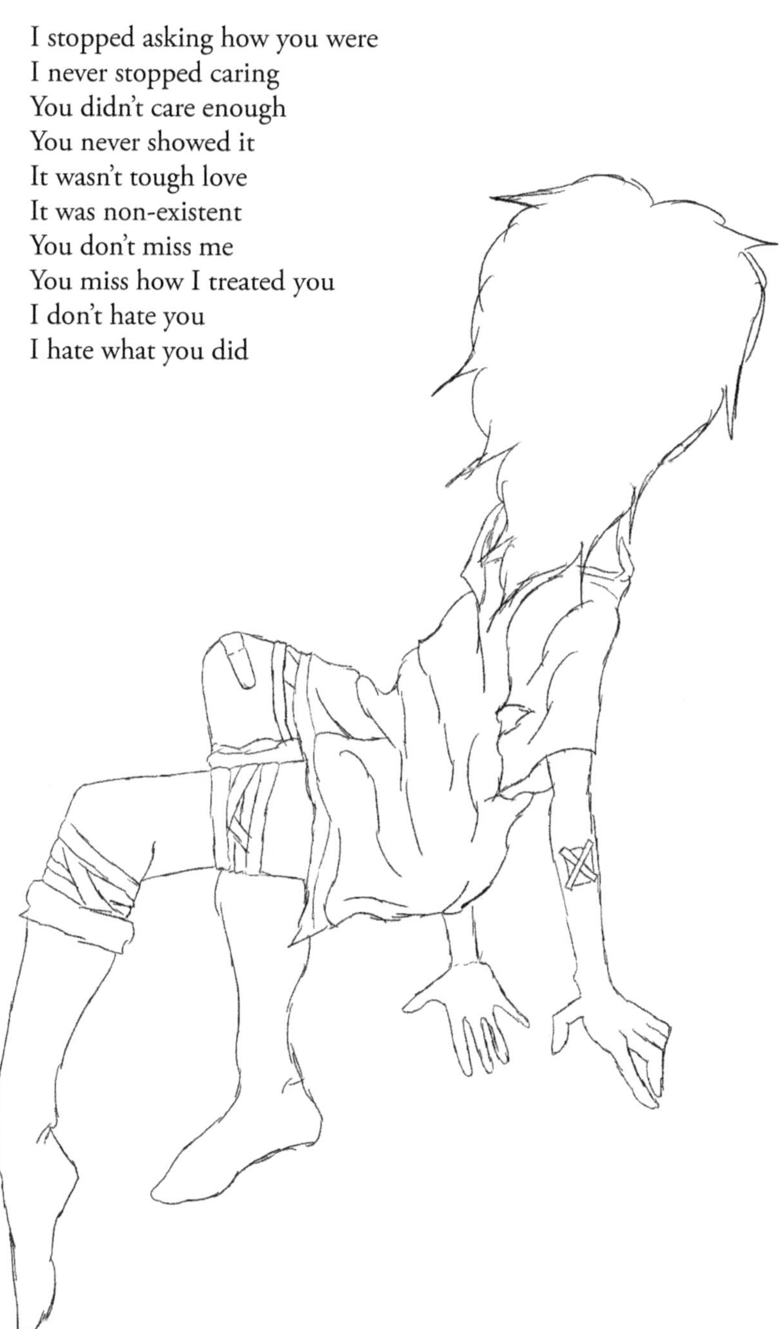

Isn’t it extraordinary
The way I break bruise and get used
Over and over again
Never learning
How I seem to refuse the lesson
It’s involuntary
So pardon my confession
But pain is my obsession
-A horribly delightful tragedy

I will always fall when I remember
All that I've lost
For I am wasted
Forced to crawl
But you love when I'm off the wall
Keeping me hidden in your prison
So when I break you can make me take the blame
Playing victim
So you can be forgiven
I'm your fallen angel turned villain
A beautiful burden to you
A marvelous sin
Hurtful and dangerous to every person

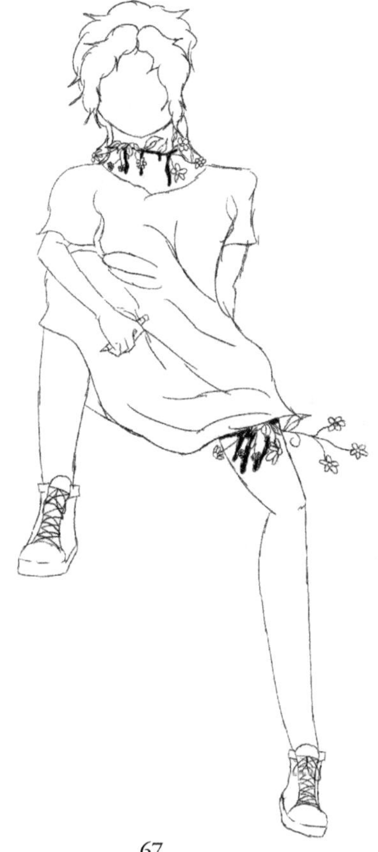

I feel like I'm always repeating the same words
But still the fog that clogs my throat
And traps the thoughts in my mind
Leaves my purpose behind
I look fine outside
My spirits are depleting inside

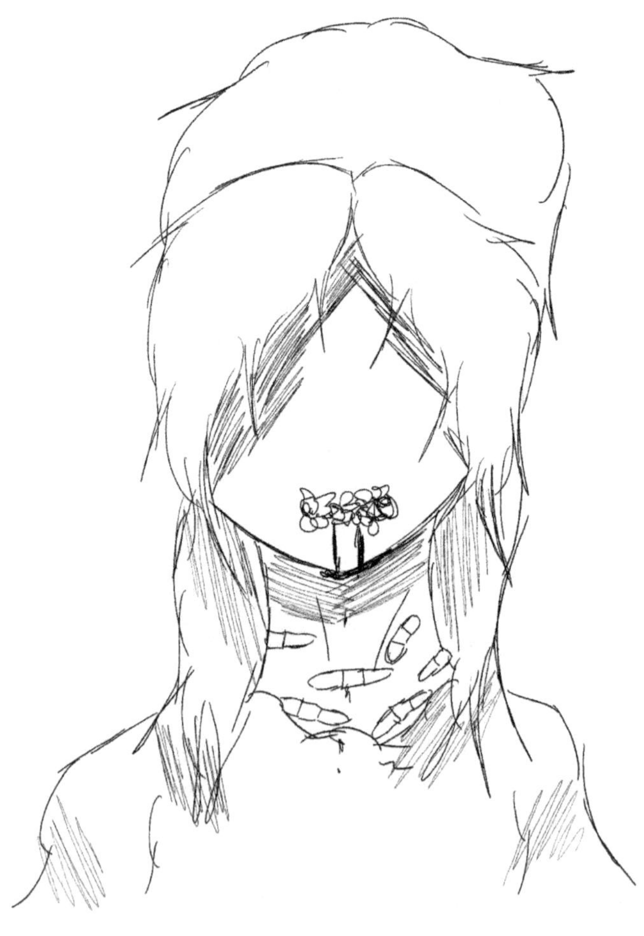

When you drown
Your head pounds
When you scream out no one will hear a sound
I've lived under the water holding my breath
Waiting for one moment to breathe again
Every ounce of me bleeding out
Fading into the waters
Turning them red
Painting the skies crimson
The noise of my own self fading slipping away
It was like the world was ending
Then there was nothing
I was nothing
And when the world started again without me
I became the loudest thing nobody could hear
I have no intent to be anything else
I'm just watching the ground beneath me crumble
Love me don't be afraid
Don't leave me I've already lost myself
Or am I found again
I'm suppressing my emotions
Pushing them deep down
Into these waters
Until they burst up and splash
Everything everywhere
It's so messy and destructive
For some reason it seems better
It seems easier to just slowly let it out
Be calmer
Bleeding out slowly and un-noticeably
It hurts more and longer
It doesn't seem healthy forcing myself to drown
Or bleed out
I'm so fond of my dangerous thoughts and parts
The struggle of getting myself to stay

My view of my body is morphed
It never looks how it actually is
Too fat too thin
It doesn't matter
It doesn't define my worth
To anyone except myself
My vision changes daily
Someone save me
This isn't healthy
Don't stop me this is what I'm used to
Found comfort in controlling my food
Who am I without this toxic mind and view
I'm helping myself it's good but I don't want to
Not ready to be healthy
I am reformed to fit what you see
I know I seem confident and independent
I'm insecure and reliant on the deals
I've made with the sick parts of my brain
See myself as a pain
Can never stand myself
Always have to be someone else
I'm wasting my breathe explaining others death

I'll slowly disintegrate from the world around me
Every conflict takes away from me
I'm chipping away slowly
Sometimes adding new pieces
I'm never me
If I'm even a thing
Not an actual person
Just a lesson you can see

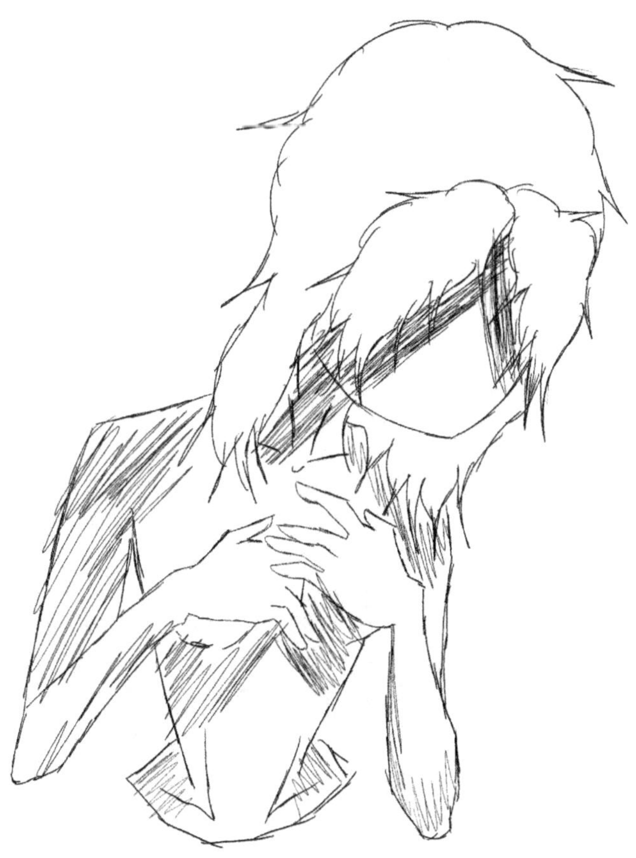

Someday when I decay
And my insides rot away
Please see me through the videos and pictures
The one you've collected throughout my life
Make me out as everything I was in your mind
Include the black and white every color inside
The good and the evil
Make me a horribly beautiful painting on an easel
An abstract art
Where it's not meant to be anything
But you can see it if you observe it close enough
That way when people hear my name
They shake their heads and say
"I wish I knew"
Even though when I tried to tell them
They didn't want to know
Maybe they'll open their eyes
My image will show them their ignorance

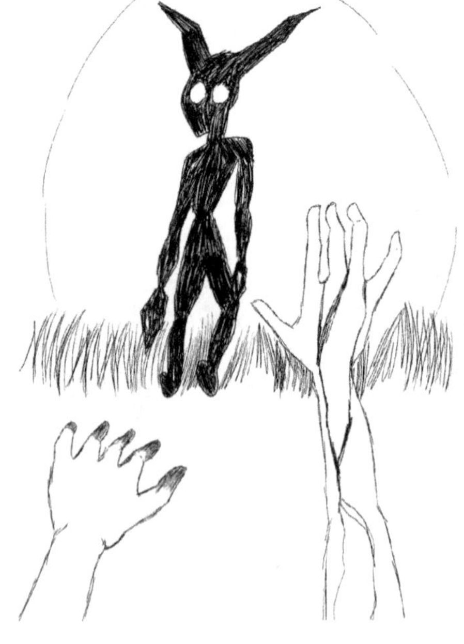

I'll make sure you never truly see
The disgusting parts of me
The parts rotten with this disease
Where I am sobbing on my knees
My fists are red and throbbing
Probably from my knuckles pounding on the floor
Blood is a possibility
I don't want to exist anymore
Existing is a task
That has become too exhausting for me
I'm not me
I'm floating in the debris
Of what I use to be
It's haunting me

I'm so sick of the person in my mirror
The one who would clench their fist
Whenever they're mad
The who opens their mouth
But never says a word
Just closes it and sighs
The person who tells me
That I am faking everything
But has seen it all
The only person
That has seen the worst of it
The fire that wishes to burn
And fuel the disgusting part of me
That I have lost
I wonder what their intention was
When they left me here
Because I've spent months searching
Pretending they're still here
They were stolen from me
The thief has left me with my grief
To mourn over the cost of feeling someone else's love
I'm never fully coming back from this robbery

My hands are covered in the red of my body
Along with everyone around me
I'm just debris from all I use to be

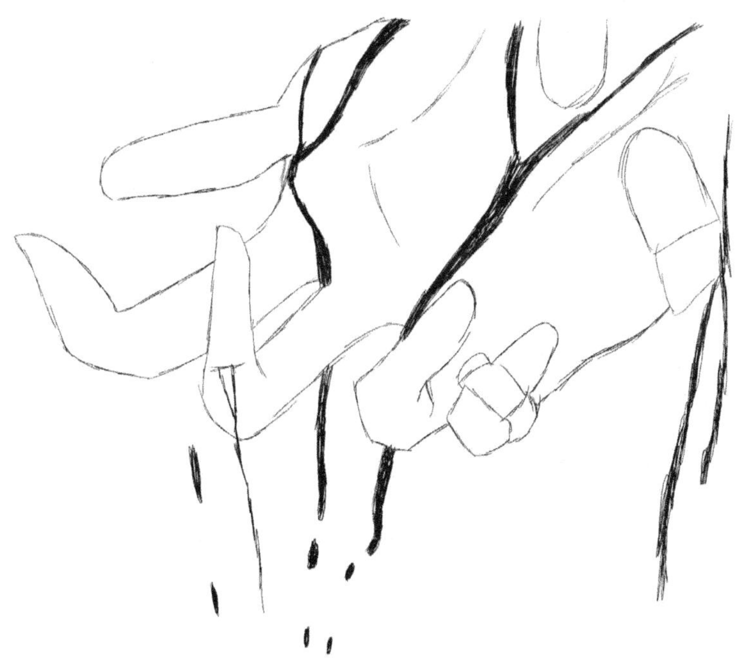

Every day is shit
Sometimes just in the morning
Sometimes just the afternoon
Sometimes all day
But never the end of the night
The end of the night is my favorite part
Of the day
Because I spend it alone
At peace
Music, drawing, writing
Just me in my purest form

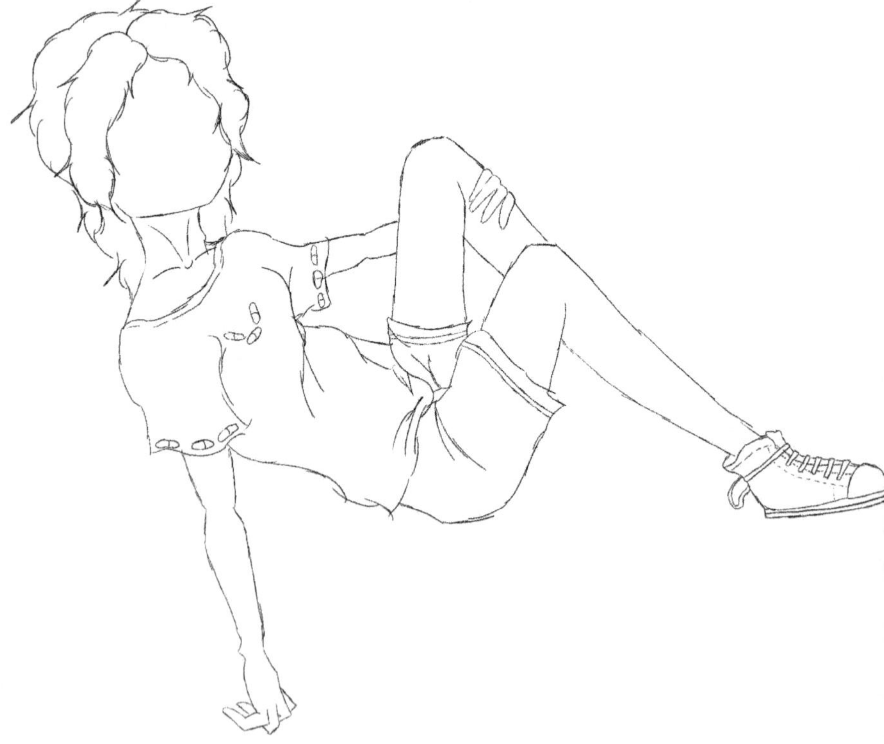

It was a sunny day one of the first of spring
Almost perfect
I was listening to a new song I liked
Walking home reflecting
I saw a squirrel
Dead on the side of the road
Her fur was all messed up
I remember stopping and staring
Seeing the death, trying to feel it
I took a picture
It seems weird
I was using the screen to prove to my mind
It was a different life
It was the part of my father's motorcycle
This was a different road
The next morning I saw it with my sister
This time her dead corpse was moved
Her unborn children lay with her
Exposed
Two deaths before their life
Before memories and love and trauma
What is it like to die before you're alive?
Do you even realize?
Would you notice if you were alive?

I don't really want to be alive right now
And I really wish I could die right now
And so what I lied about
How I'm really feeling inside my mind
But I really wish that I could run away and hide
Maybe I should just lie down
Try to figure this out
Or I could sleep
And put it off, become wasted on my dreams
But then it'd get carried out for eternity
Now I'm down
On my knees and no one can hear me.

I finally came up with a solution to all my problems
I simply won't exist
I'll bleed out after I slit my wrists
Blow my brains
Hang my name
Take some meds
Drown and never be seen again
This will start a new problem
I'll never know who I could've been

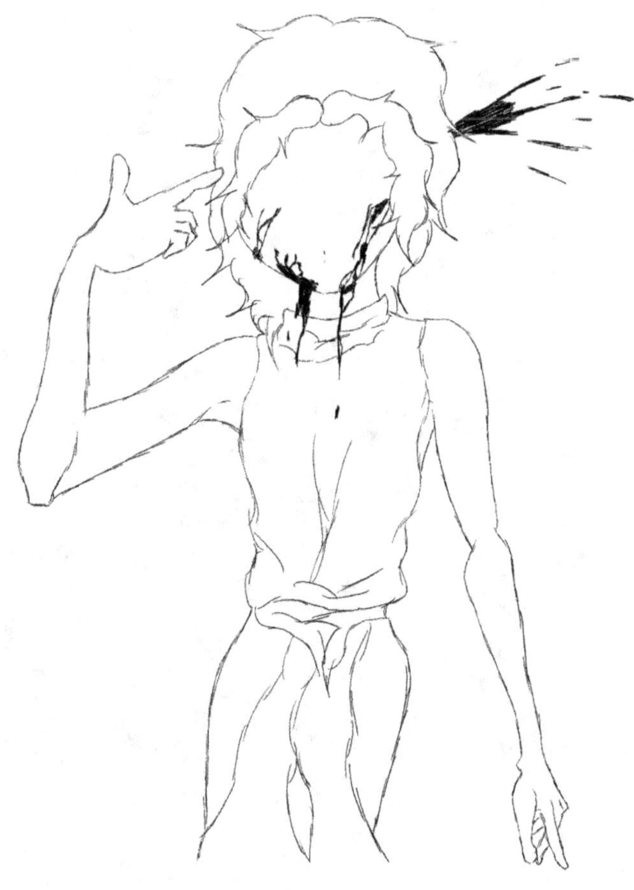

There's a Sun Hidden Behind the Clouds

Experimental
Used for perfection that
You'll never receive

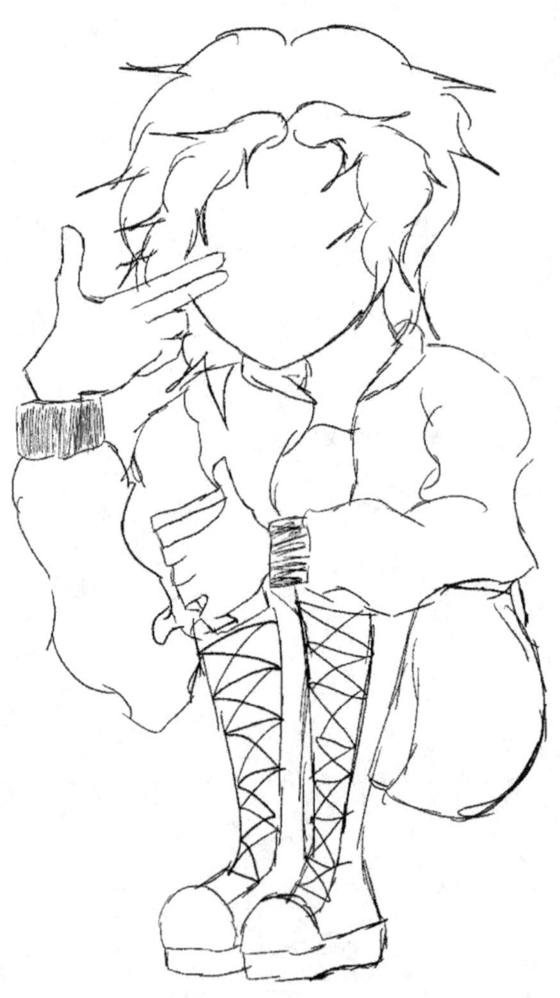

It’s temporary
My trauma is only a minute for you
It’s a millennia for me

Are you scared of what you created?
I haven’t done anything yet

I'm not real

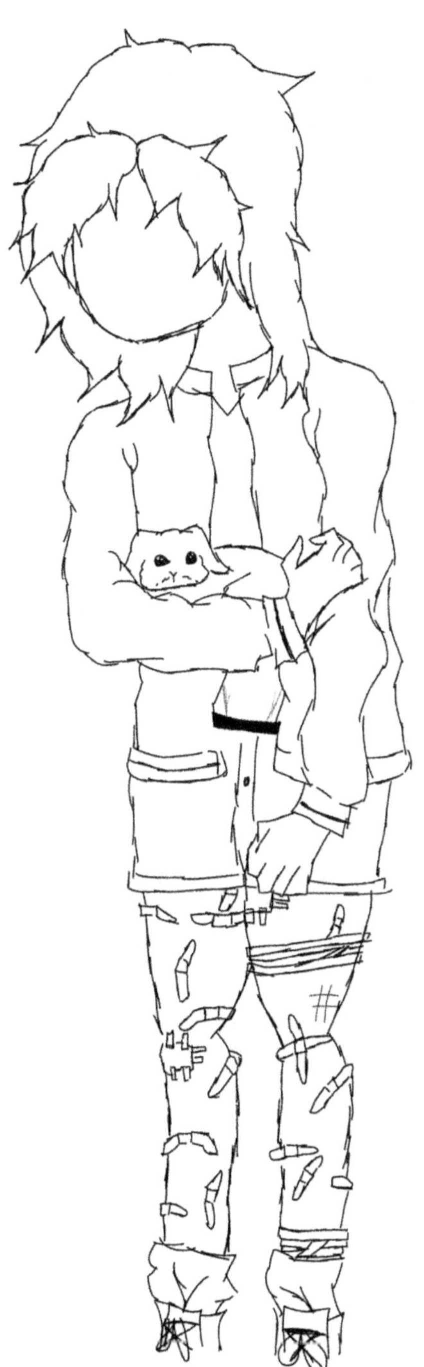

Everyone wants to help the villain
After hearing their story
But that doesn't mean the villain needs anyone
That's what makes them dangerous

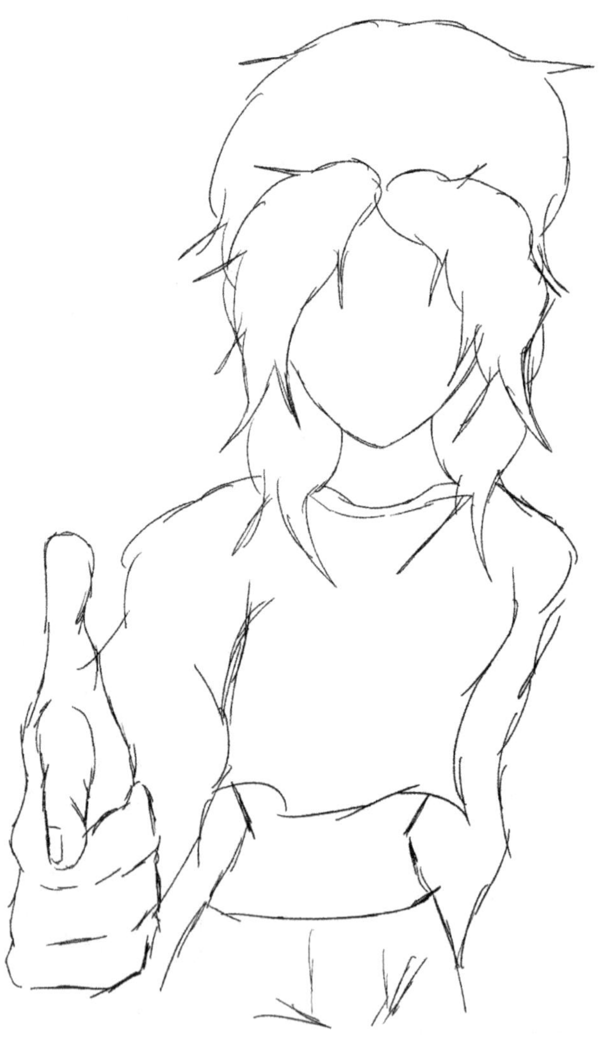

You made me feel whole
But I never needed you
So why do you keep it as a threat?

You can very easily break a vase
It shatters so quickly
But it took so long to build and paint
To actually make it a vase
Your stomach churns and aches with quilt
So you apologize
But the vase is still broken
And even with the glue
There are still cracks
It becomes more fragile
Now you don't truly understand
What you do
Until you realize
That trust is like a vase
Holding the flowers
And sweet water of a bond
That you swore
You wouldn't break

Don't get to know me
Until you hear about me
I'll screw you over
I'll be there and then dump you
While screaming about how you hurt me
Cower at every bullet
But face the gun
Then shoot you with a toy one
It will welt your skin and sting your blood
I'll fuck everything up

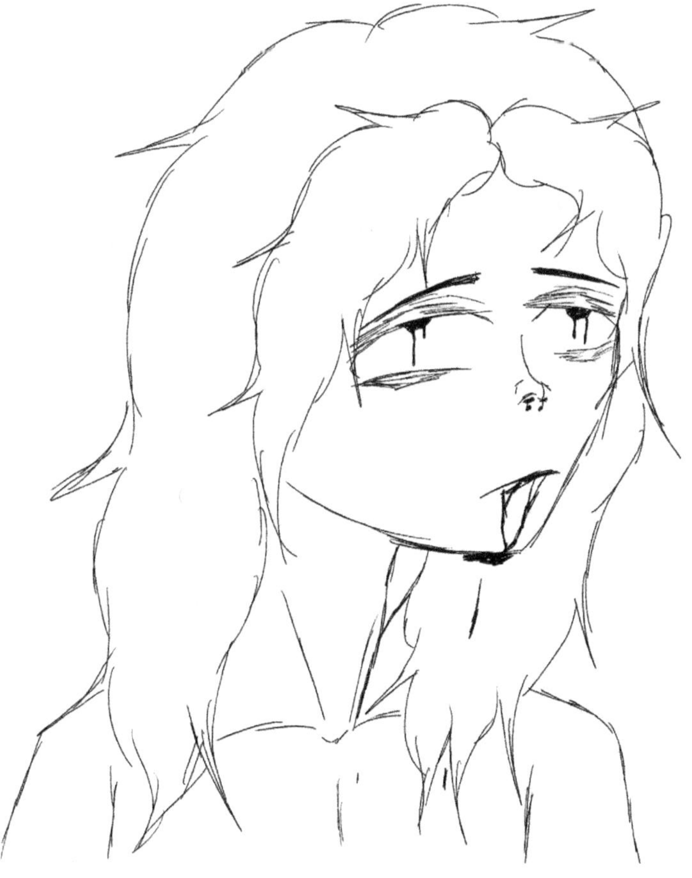

I hate the cold
But can't stand drinking hot tea
It can be inside me but never around me

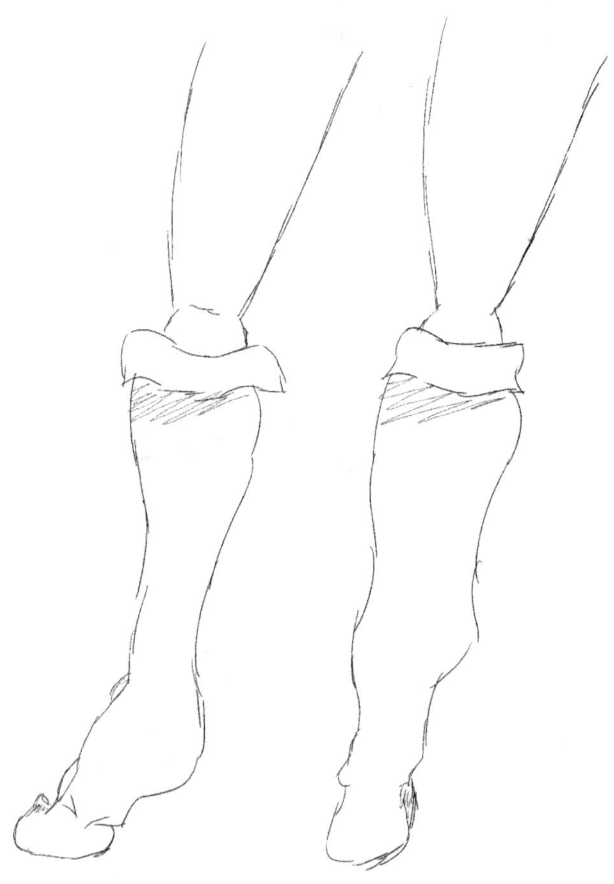

Toxic friendship is what starts good
It'll slowly fade into a dark gray
You will whine and complain for days
Before you finally say
This isn't right
Then you decide to test them
See if they'll put up a fight
Disappointed to realize
They aren't willing to give the same effort as you
Now it's up to you
To leave or stay
For somebody you mean nothing to

We tear the Earth apart
We created the word monster
To make ourselves seem superior
To hide the wrong doings
This treachery is brewing
And it is worse than Australian fires
We are going to be the next
Michael Myers
Our worst enemies are each other
Younger generations scream out about
Pride joy and equality
Our beliefs and how to fix what is broken
Mend and love
They're are told they are stupid and sensitive
That they haven't been broken enough
By this cruel place we call home
That they are dramatic claiming they're so alone
No we've been broken
Beaten around pushed to the ground
We just never lost our spirit
We've realized what we want
Someone to call our bluff
We are acting so strong while our knees tremble
We are waiting for our worlds to crumble
We feel so deeply
Because everyone around us is beating down on us
And we know the world is ending
We are trying to enlighten you
Not forsaken your generation
So please listen to me, to us
When we tell you this
Just because you're older
Does not mean you're wiser

Everything you do is justified
Until somebody does it to you

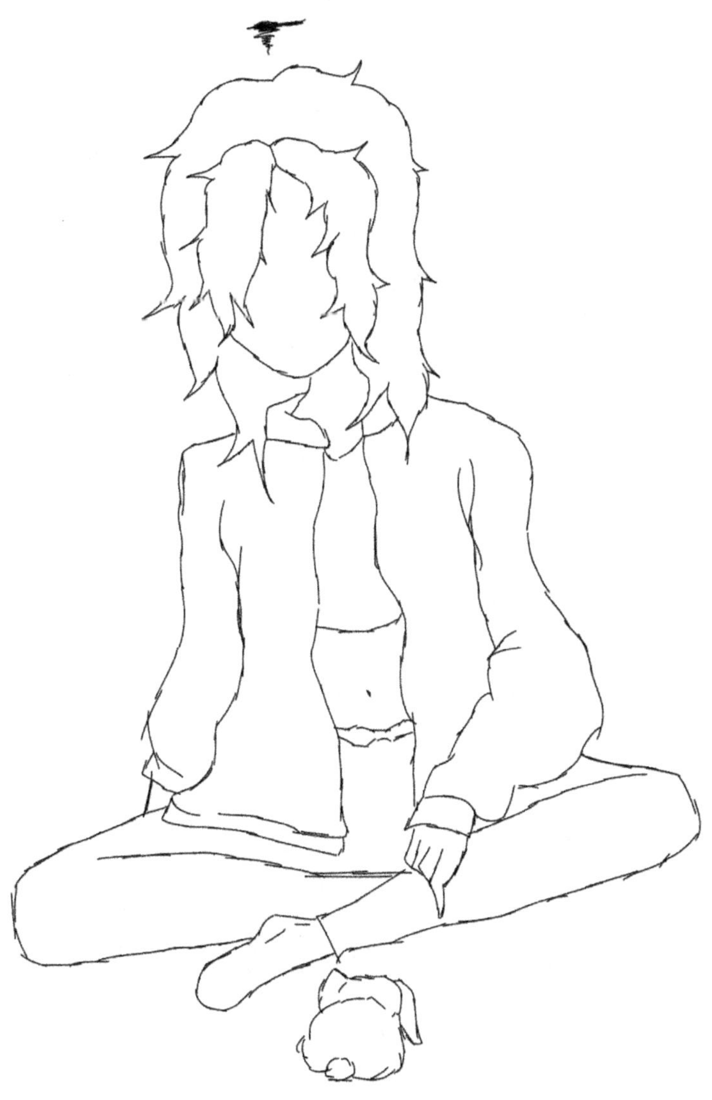

You can't trust me to save you
I am half diseased
Dying, decaying, breaking
From my own poison
If you're not careful, and you never are
You might catch it too

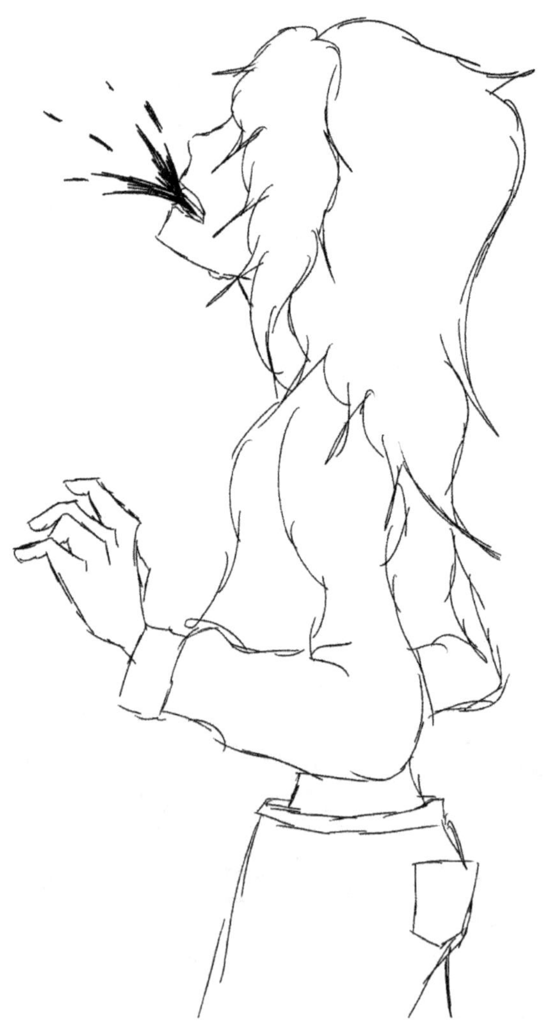

My illness will never shape me
What part of me is left
Which parts are me
Which part is my sickness

Run from your problems
Without a plan
It's the illusion of freedom
Without peace

I don't want to be quiet anymore
You took everything
Why is this something only I can see?

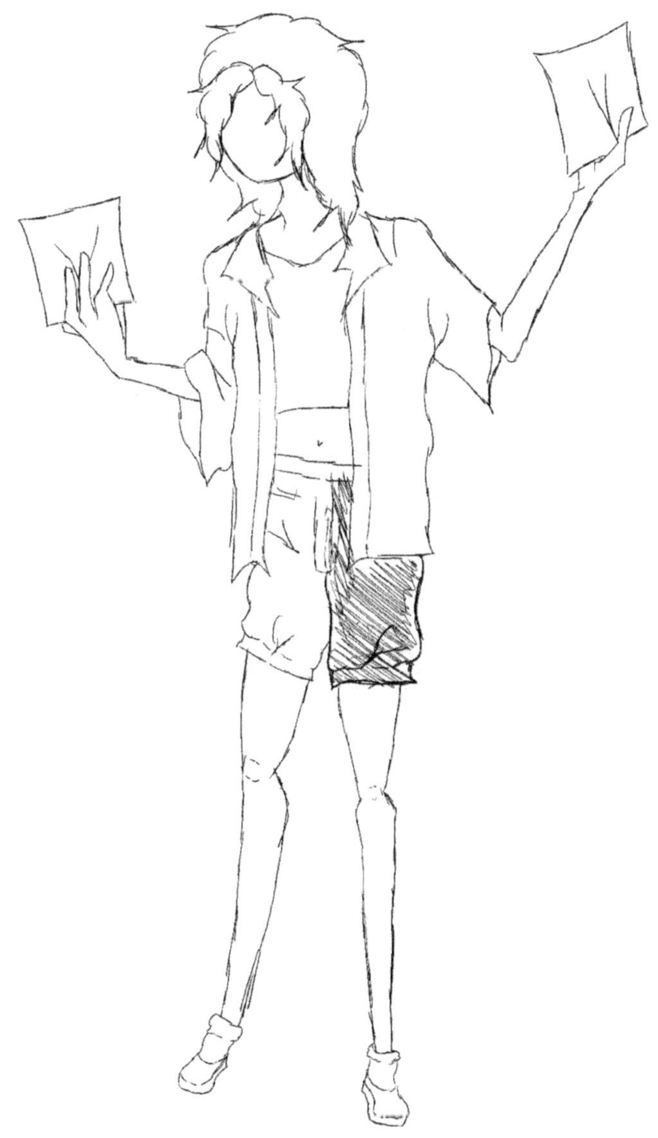

I feel different from my reflection
Like someone else with the same scars as me
But their face and body doesn't fit me
Something isn't right
Everything is wrong
My reflection isn't me

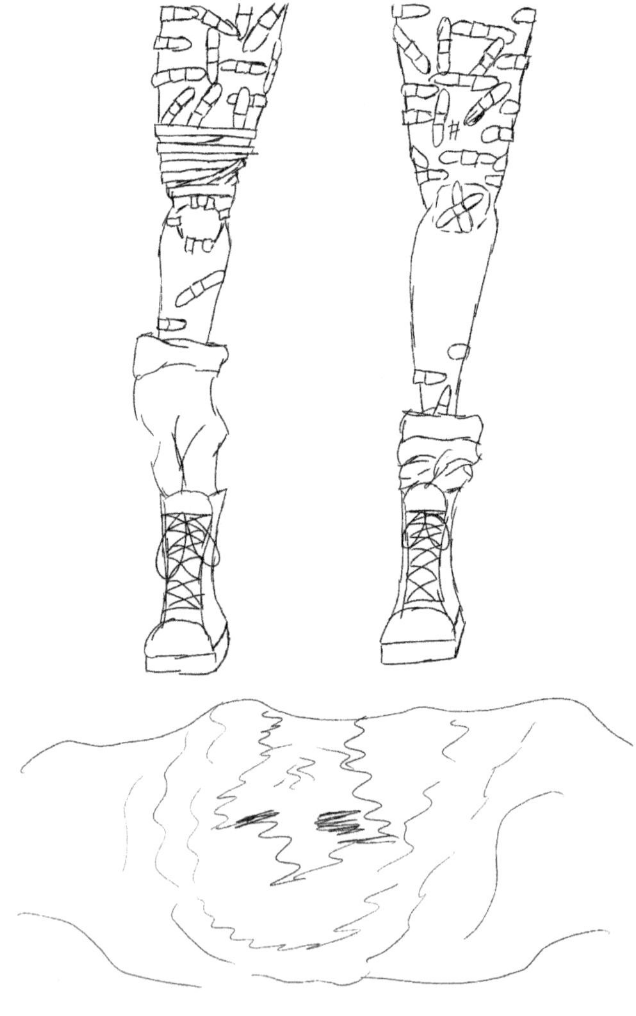

How did you make me forget my place so easily?
Saw myself as a disgrace
Felt misplaced
I preached that everyone is equal
We all bleed red
Our tears are salty and our eyes dreary
I forgot to see myself the same way
I wasn't bleeding red
I was bleeding a golden yellow that looked so pretty
It glowed
The words you chose reminded me
I'm only pretty when I'm broken and bleeding
They haunted me in my mirror
Taunting me
I couldn't see straight

If you care so much why don't you try showing it
Are you scared?
Or is it just easier to lie to my face
And receive my care

I can no longer ignore the gory parts of life
I've grow more curious than before
I feel the need to explore
See what it's like
To experience every inch of pain and relief
Is it real?
How real can it be?
Too real?
Will it make me real?

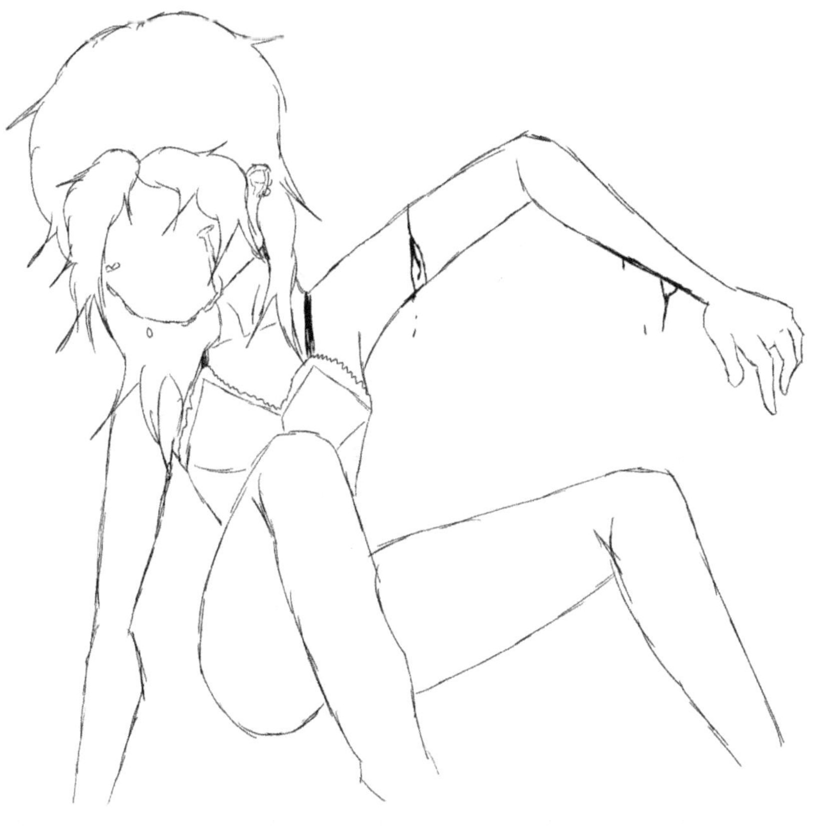

Would you like me more if my smile were wider
My eyes brighter
My body lighter
My halo tighter
Cutting off the circulation to my brain
So I'll be the same

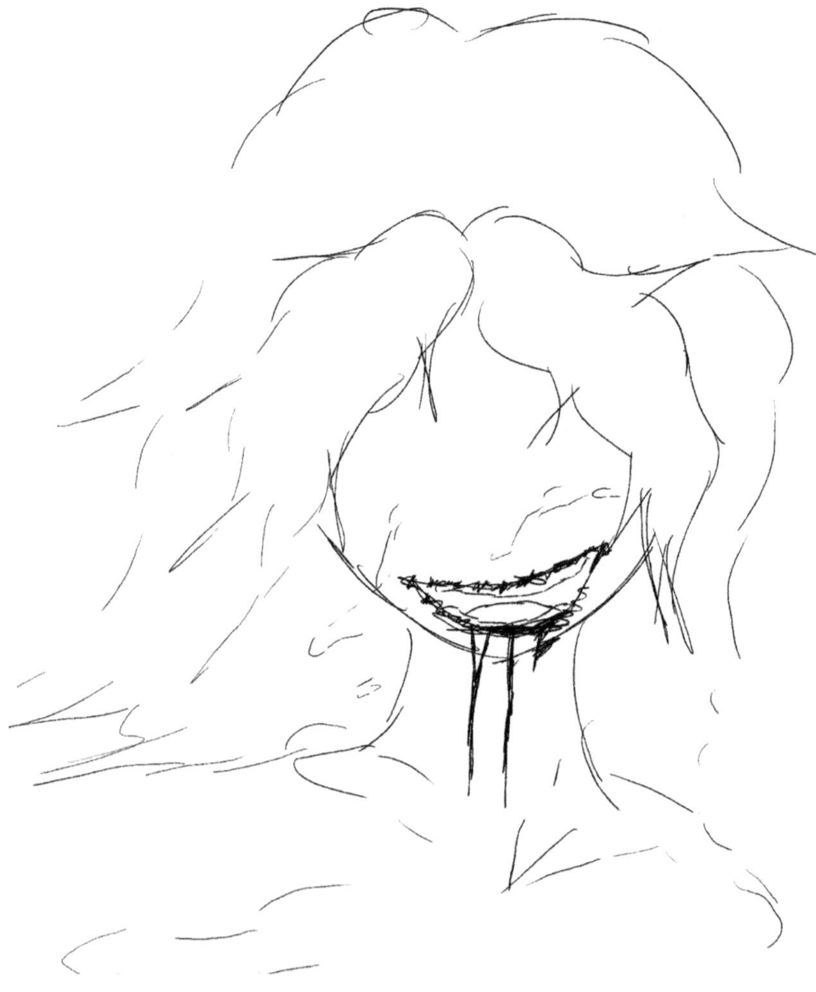

I'm delusional
From all of your
Overused illusions

I’ve spent a lifetime crying over you
Choking over your words
While they hung in the air
The way you claimed you cared
I die each time I remember our long nights
The mornings after the fights
I was never right

Do you enjoy watching the pain you cause
Since it's not your loss

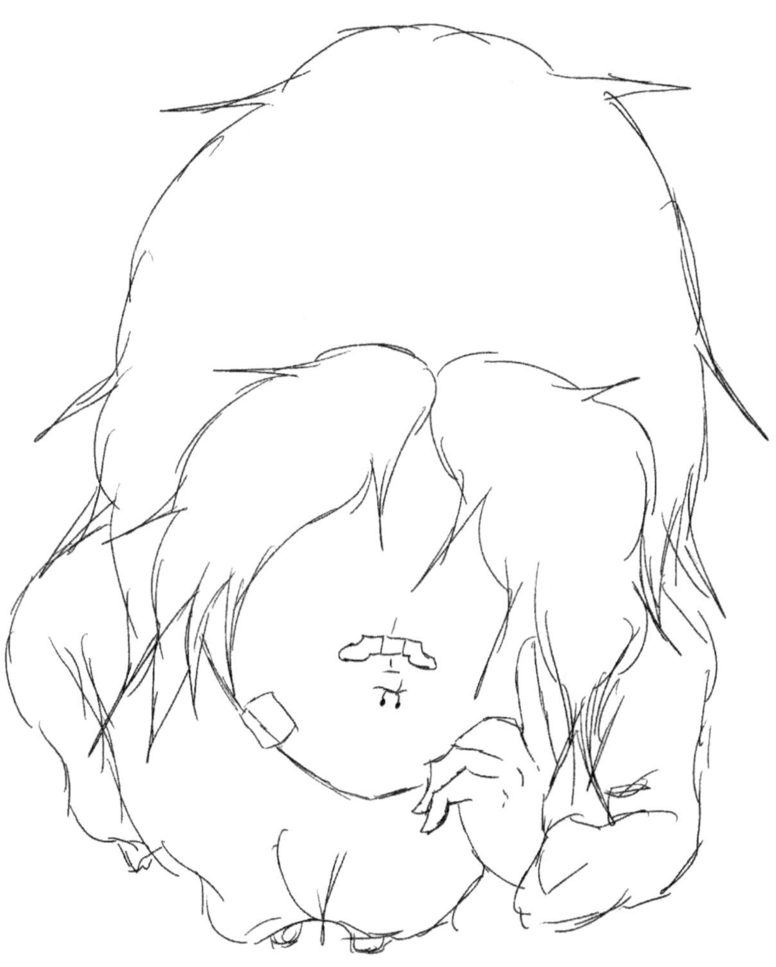

When someone realizes their words are a weapon
They will use them for multiple things
Healing themselves and others
Hurting themselves and others
Defending themselves and others
Enjoying themselves and the company of others
And expressing themselves
All of these will be art
And it'll be a beautiful blood shed

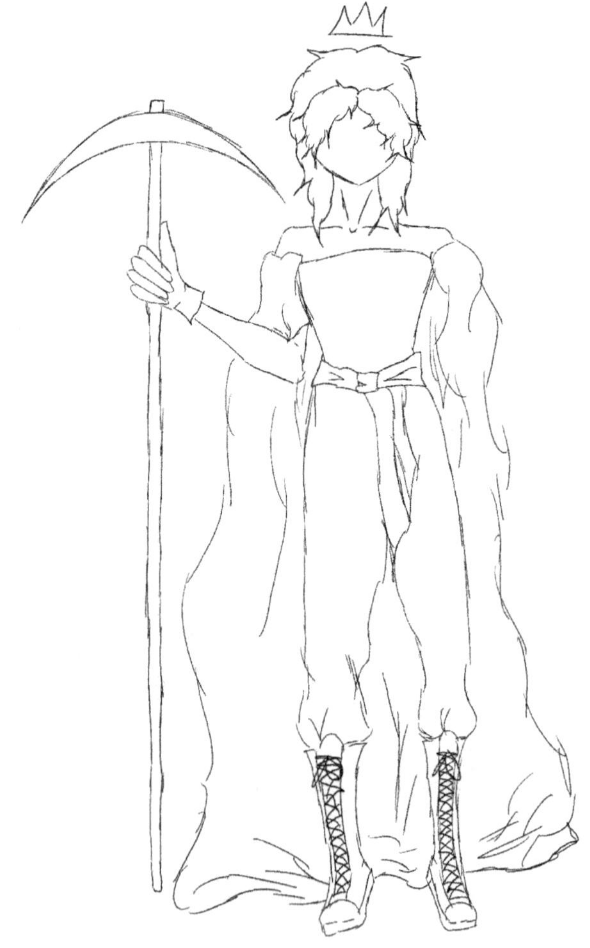

The most pure form of pain
Is what is screamed and cried over
The kind where you destroy
Yourself and everything around you
The most unclear form of pain
Is expressed as anger
They both look the same

An eternity of sleep
Some peace at last
A fire turned to ash
No more blood to bleed
Everyone's equal love received
My lungs permanently deflated
Should have never waited
To listen to all the thoughts I use to mask

So long as I bend for you I am worth the universe
But if I snap and reverse my wounds
Healing from the damage you do
Then refuse to take the abuse
Once I am no longer of use
The only thing I am worthy of
Is the loss that comes with love

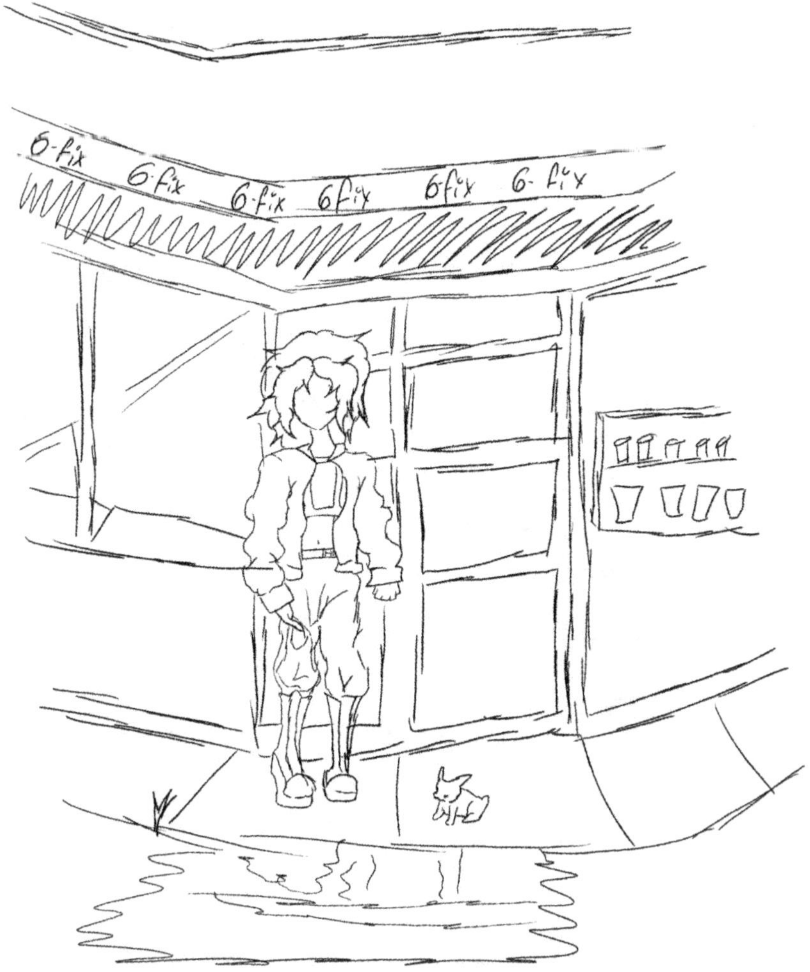

Everybody wants what they don't have
I need what I can never reach

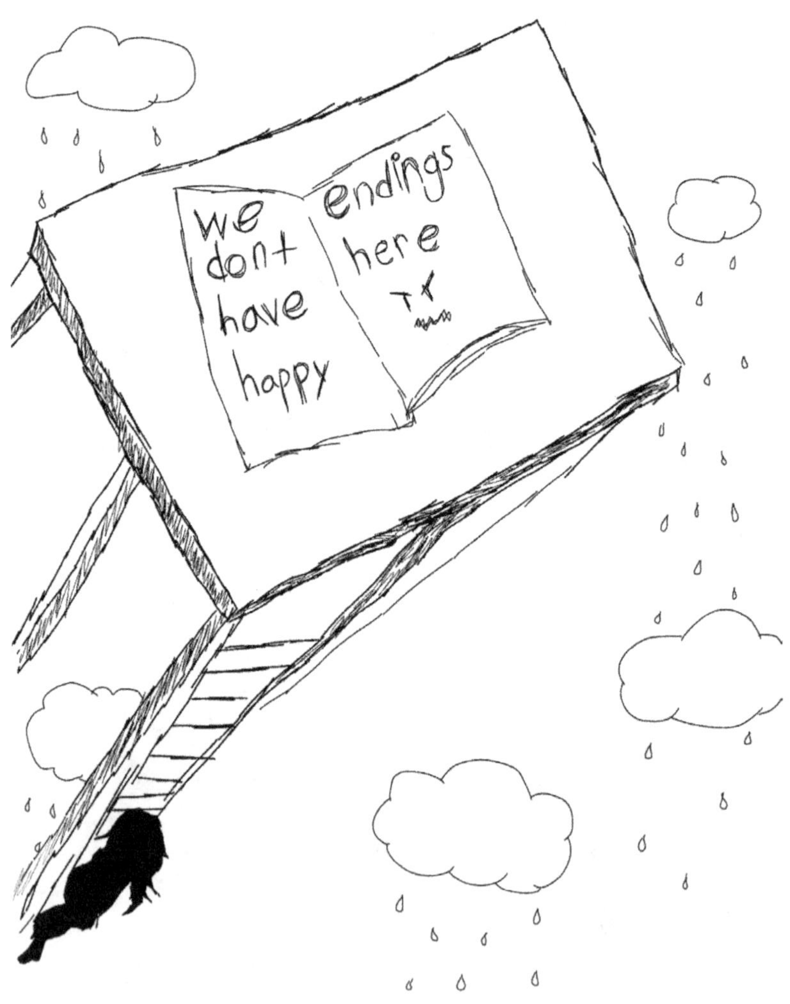

I don't normally act on my rage
I learned how to turn that off at an early age
But you
Oh you have brought out a different part of me
One my family can never seen
You make me lose control
Luckily I have your number blocked on my phone
Had to erase and lock away every memory
Any trace of you
But how unfortunate for you to be such a fool
That you would wander back into my life
Some place that was never
Meant to hold you

How could you sit and listen to my pain
Then stab me while I was in vain
Because of what you did
Somehow you're still the victim of all of it
Not saying I'm better or you're to blame
Just that we aren't the same
That I'm no liar
Willing to admit the shots I fired

"I promise"
What an easy lie
My eyes burn from the salt in their sockets
I left our notes in my coat pocket
Washed the blood from the sleeves
How could the paper shred and the words leave
It was an accident
I promise

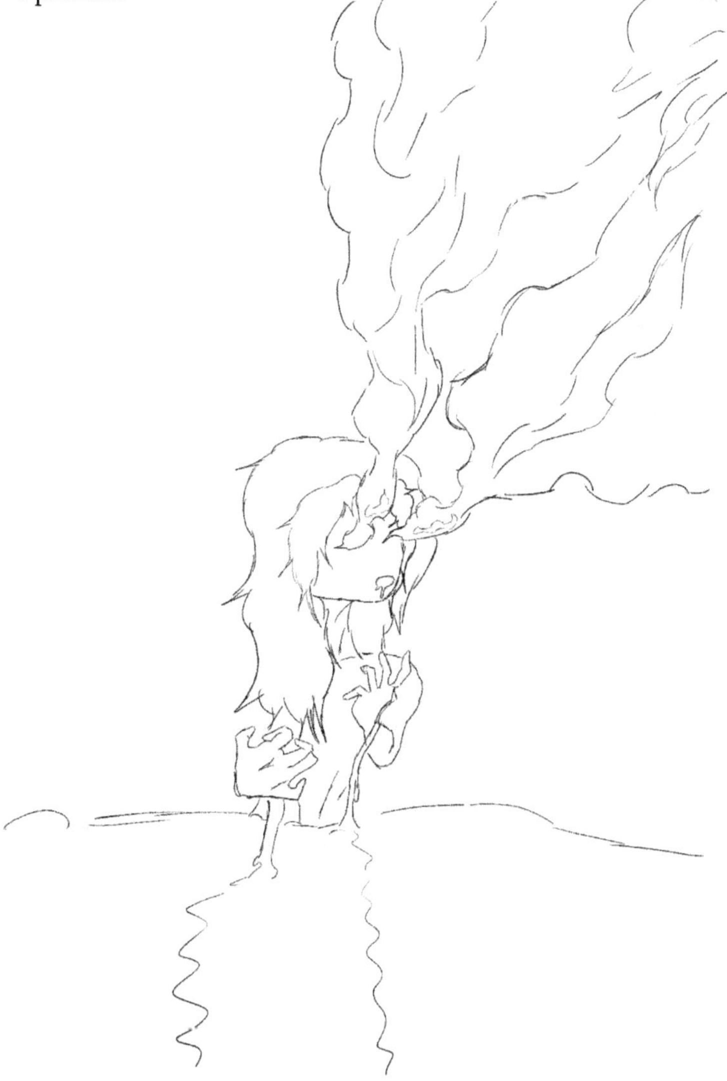

We wish upon everything
From shining and falling stars
To flowers we call weeds
Blow to spread their seeds
Their growth granting us greed
Coins dropping into the water
We are so desperate not to accept reality

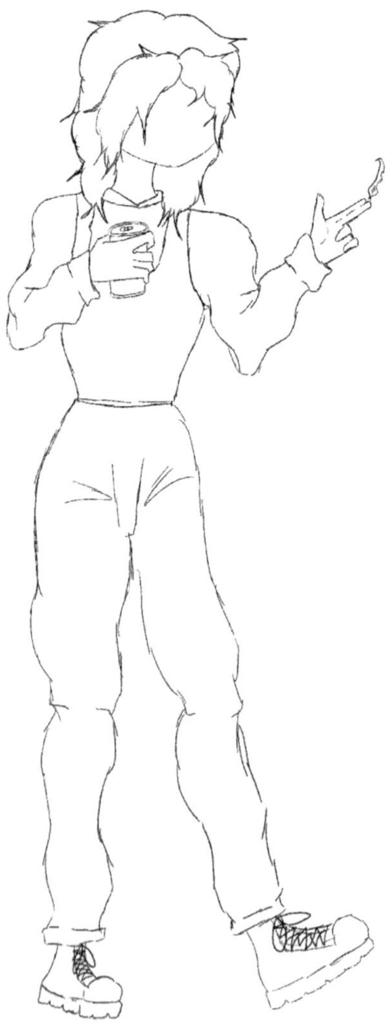

"If god is real you'd be an angel"
Funny for you to say such a thing
When you don't believe in god
And neither do I
But I still loved hearing those words
Masking the truth
Your lies seemed so beautiful in my eyes
Just how you claimed you loved my design
You loved it so much
That it would rot in your touch

Lately
My fantasies
Have been absolutely flooded
With all the wonderful ways for me to bleed
My trauma is controlling me
I don't mean to mislead
But I don't think you're very good for me

I'm weighing down my reality
Thinking and questioning everything I've ever seen
Or ever heard
I want to believe in something further than before
I don't want to participate in this lifetime anymore

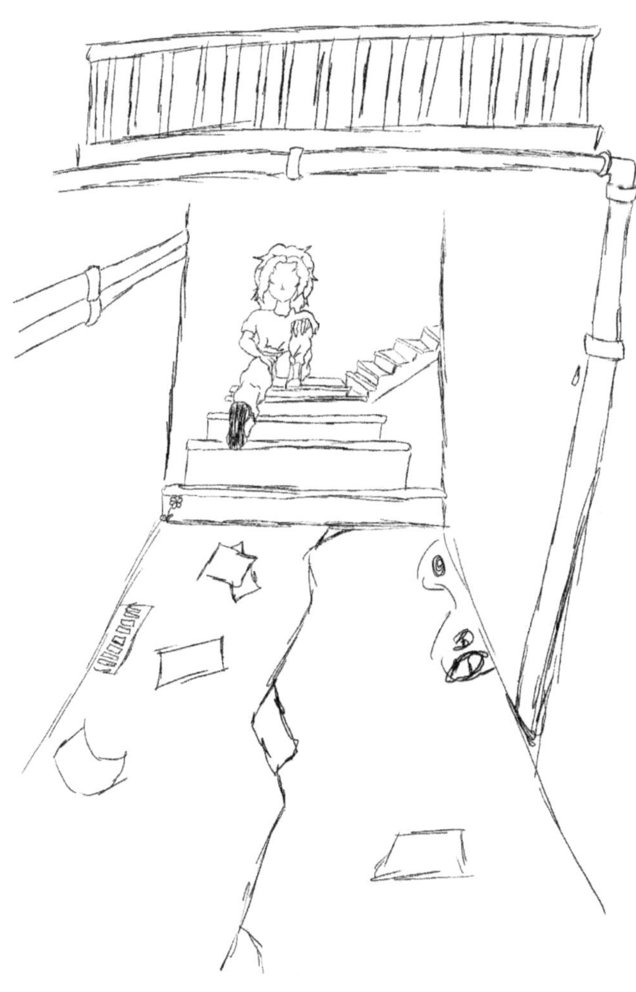

Don't laugh until you know you're safe
Never stop looking back
Learn from every mistake
Expect history to repeat itself
Always know where you're going
Everything's the same
You'll never be safe

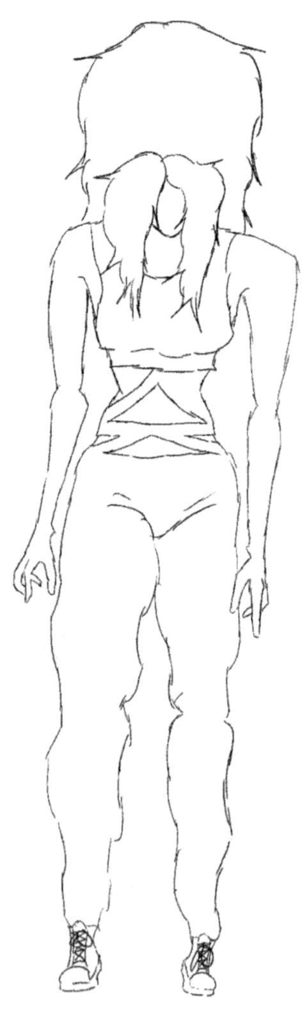

I am not the person I claim to be
Not as strong and powerful
As I portray myself to be
I am a sad shitty pity party
A show of mishaps and misery
Snap-backs and coming back rising
Once again
From the dead
A fraud fake and phony
Incapable of holding the same single identity
Allow me to introduce the new me
While I burn everything I use to be

The story of a phoenix

I've always been jealous of people
Who seemed to enjoy life more than me
Those who had control of their peace
One day it hit me
After my reality came crashing around me
I was stuck in my head from my unmet needs
I found myself but lost my will
To fill the world around me
With things that will keep me
It's concerning
The way I am learning that I am unwell
No one had control
They just knew how to feel and live
So much more deeply
I knew how to but lacked the experience
For my elders guidance left me untouched
By the simple joys
But it was soon destroyed by my burning traumas
Leaving me for ash
My perseverance torn in half
Felt alone
Made so others would know
I am writing this for you
You are not alone your power is there
Hiding and unknown
There are so many like you
But not everyone is capable of doing it the way you do
Make your power known I'd like to hear you too

When I was young I spent so much time
Pretending to move things with my mind
Never realized the power of creativity
This escape from reality
My ability to rewrite my fake destiny
So it suits me
The story lines parallel to my life time
Daydream all the time
When I was young
When I needed someone I turned to my imagination
Creative stories where someone
Had everything I wanted
So when I meet my accomplishments
It doesn't seem real
I can't accept something I don't deserve
It's absurd for me
To think I could be anything but a fantasy
I'm trapped in this daze
My world is my stage
So fake and yet it's my reality
I can't feel my own emotions
Even though I had them
It's a simple answer truly
I am not real

When you called me bad
You meant yourself
When you said I'm like you
You meant the old you
The one that was left untouched by your fury
When you said you'd give me everything
You meant nothing
When you said you loved me
You meant you hardly liked me
But your love was forced by instinct
When you said we don't talk anymore
You meant I drifted away
And you weren't wrong
When I said you made me
The happiest I've ever been
I lied like you did

My time in this world is limited
I want to spend it un-contained unbothered
Yet I'm constantly battling my paranoia
Check every door
Think of every possible scenario
Every single escape
Planned into my mind
This is the world I've been raised in

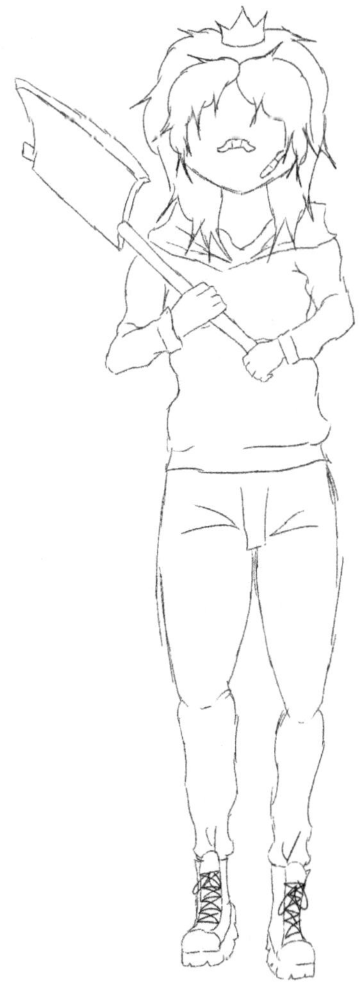

I always hold on
When I should let go
And because of this
I always let go
When I should hold on

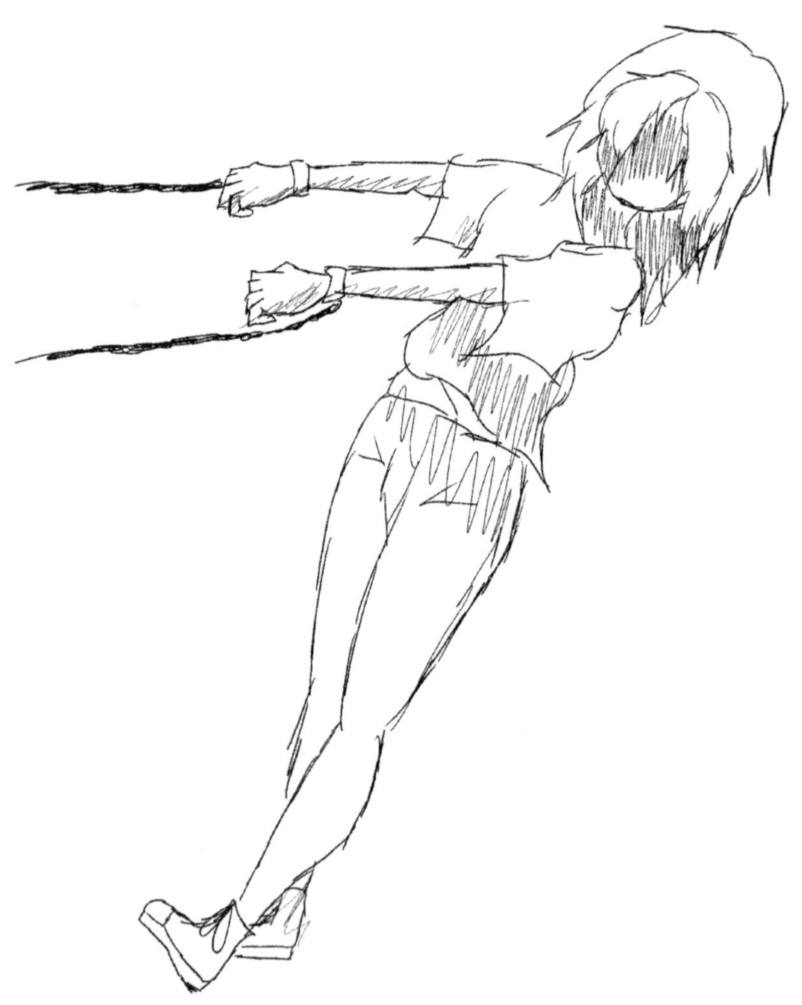

What would you do if I disappeared?
You don't even notice when I'm here
Even though you need me
I need to flee
Don't try and find me
I need this for myself
I can't be your perfect baby anymore
Am I selfish?

Fun fact about me
I am immune to poison ivy
But attracted to toxic relationships
I'm like a magnet to anything
And everything that'll hurt me
Taking up problems I can't solve
My little brother
Always picks up the biggest sticks
The ones he can use as weapons
But he can't hold and control them
I take the biggest problems
Wrapping my brain around them
That's where I get all this
So called wisdom from
Mature for my age
Always so certain but I'm so lost
Stuck in my thoughts
My mind is a post apocalyptic stage
I'm wandering in the damage
That's been done to my brain
Walls are built out of all the dead things
Dreams that have crashed
Hope that's been killed off
Only because I always bite off
More than I can chew
So much so that I can't bare to eat food
It makes me sick
Something else is in control of it

I never knew it was something bad
How could it be so horrible if it felt so right
In my mind it's always night
But not the bad kind
The kind where the streets are lit up by neon lights
The stars are out and so bright
Where music plays in every alley
Where everything seems peaceful but unsettling
A place made for certain types of people
I've always enjoyed things
That turned my stomach
And made it ache
I say I hate it but I always wander back
So I must love it

You know it took me a long time
But I finally read you
You've been neglected your whole life
So you decided to try and invest yourself
Into people who over-loved you
You pushed the limits
When you didn't really care about it
You just loved the way that it felt
So you emptied them all
Pouring out every single liquid
In their jar
Tell me how far did we go
Traveling down the road
Was that the longest anyone lasted
Have I held it out the most
Did you enjoy it?
Taking from me I mean
I never wanted to stop
But I question if it was ever meant to start
It was fun while it lasted

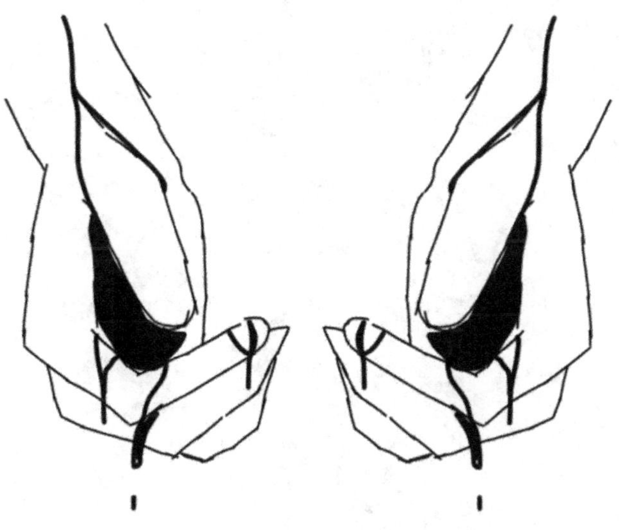

Planting
Seeds

I'm only self-centered now that I say
"Fuck you"
Instead of
"Fuck me"

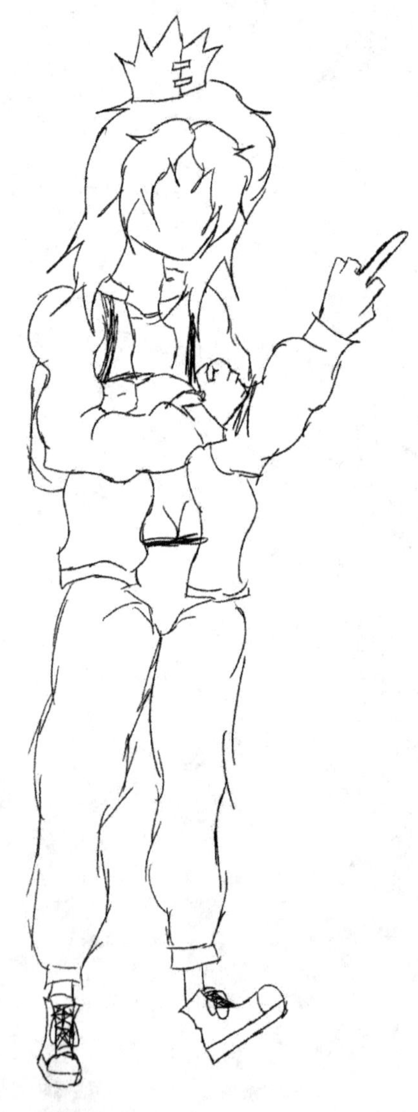

Break me
Take me
To a place where I can
Think of how to love myself

I'll call you later
Another promise you broke
But this time instead of crying
I mourned you instead

I want you to hurt the way you made me hurt
But I
Don't want to hurt you

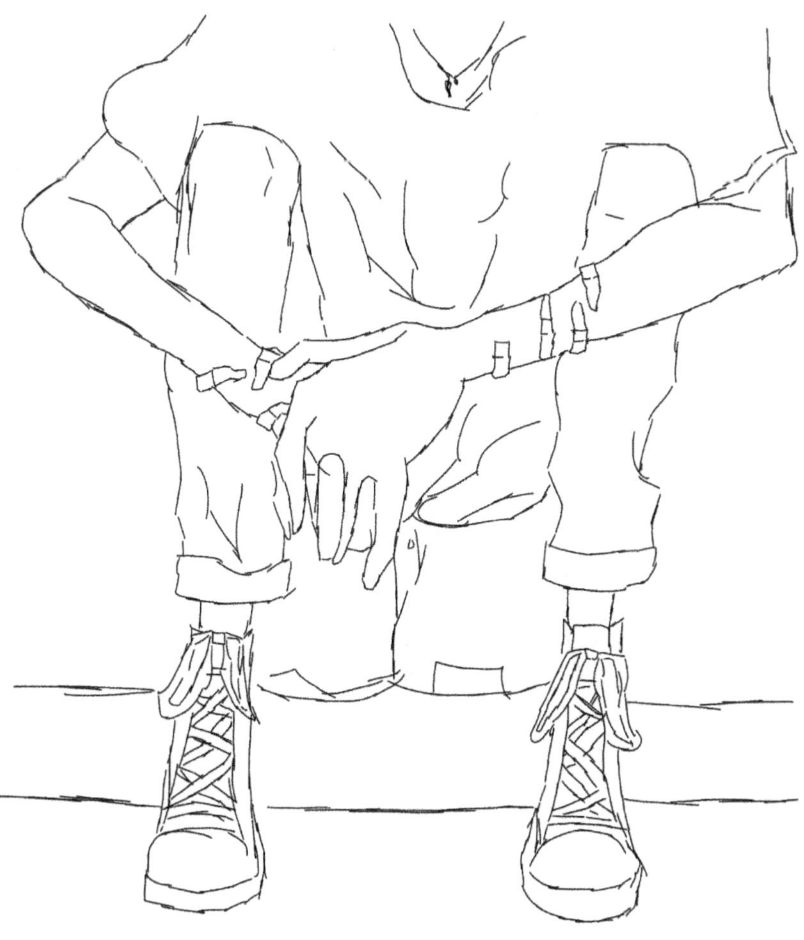

All the memories I have to make without you
Are the ones that hurt the most

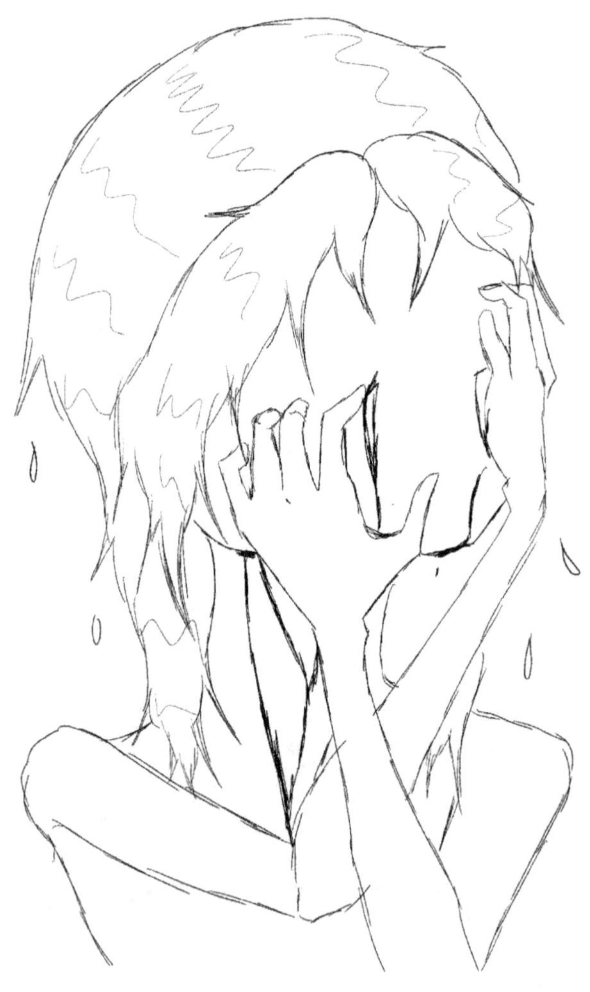

I refuse to be quiet
Why can't you hear me?

I’m not strong
I’m incapable of quitting
It’s a weakness

Forgive me
This isn't the real me
But the air is too toxic
And it stings my lungs
I think I forgot how to breathe

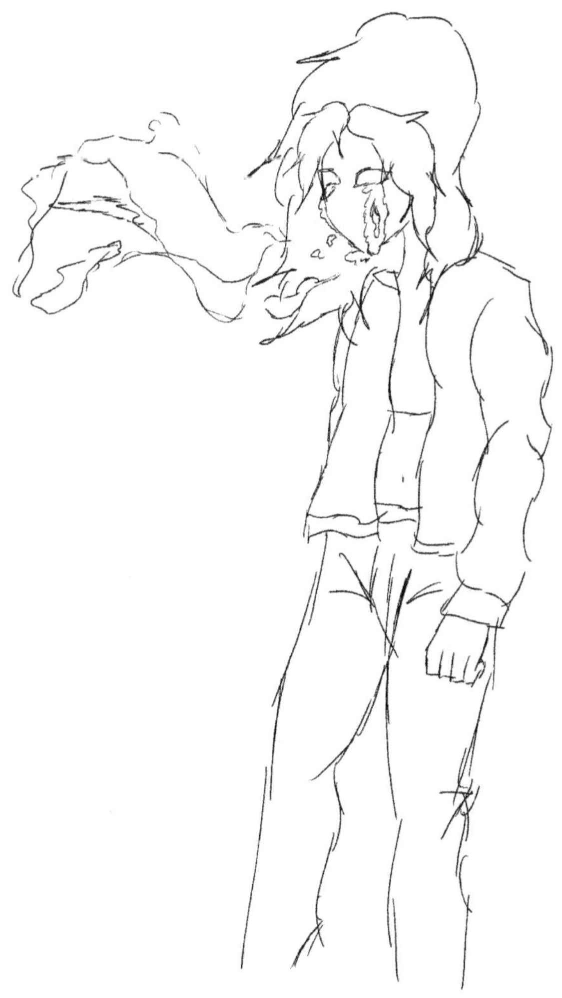

I've discovered everything
I know nothing

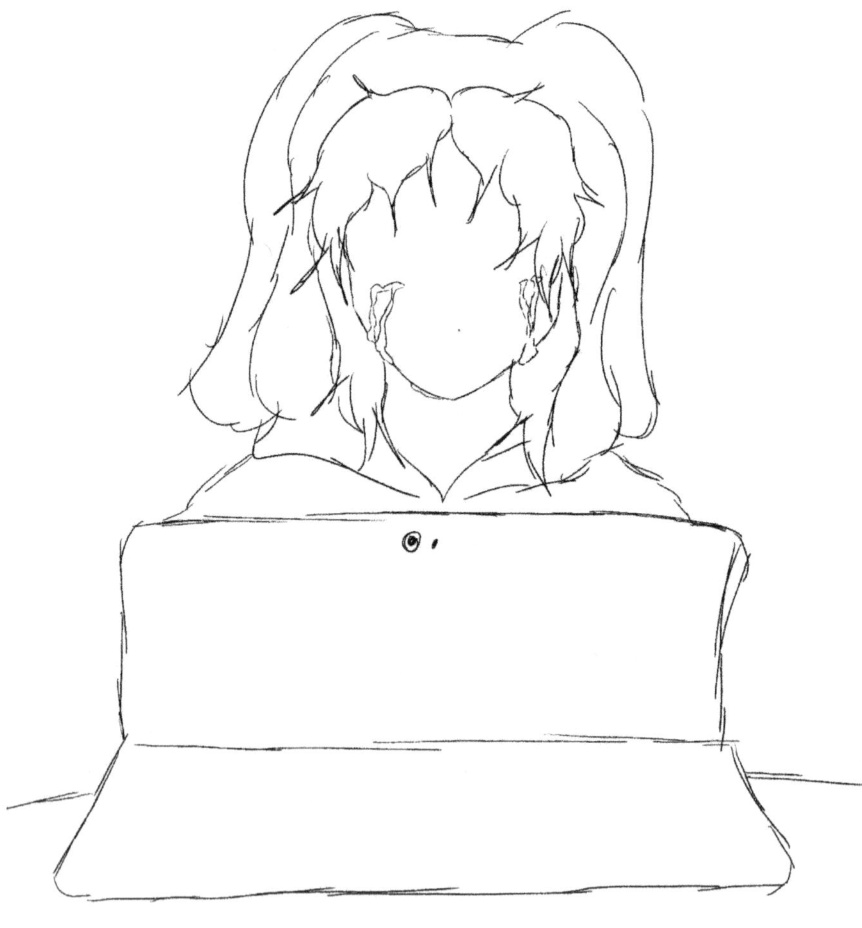

Hide your problems
But still complain

If this is what you call
Caring
Then I don't want
To be cared about anymore

I rather be nobody
Then satisfy your beliefs
Of what I should be

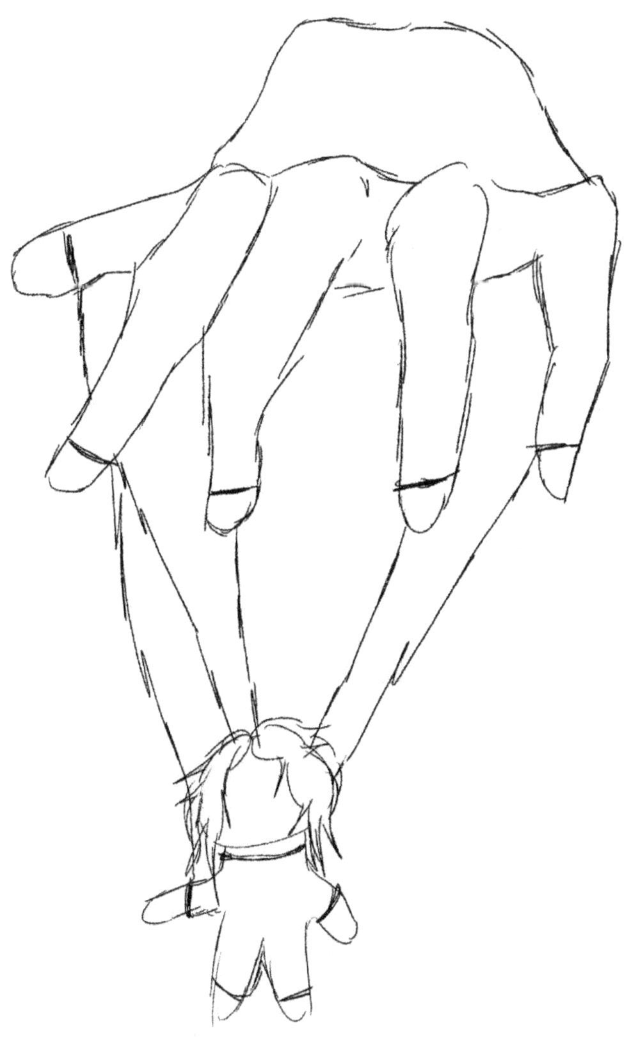

Trying to survive
Changed and got revived
What'll you do?
Cry over the me you lose?
I've already lost more than you had to offer

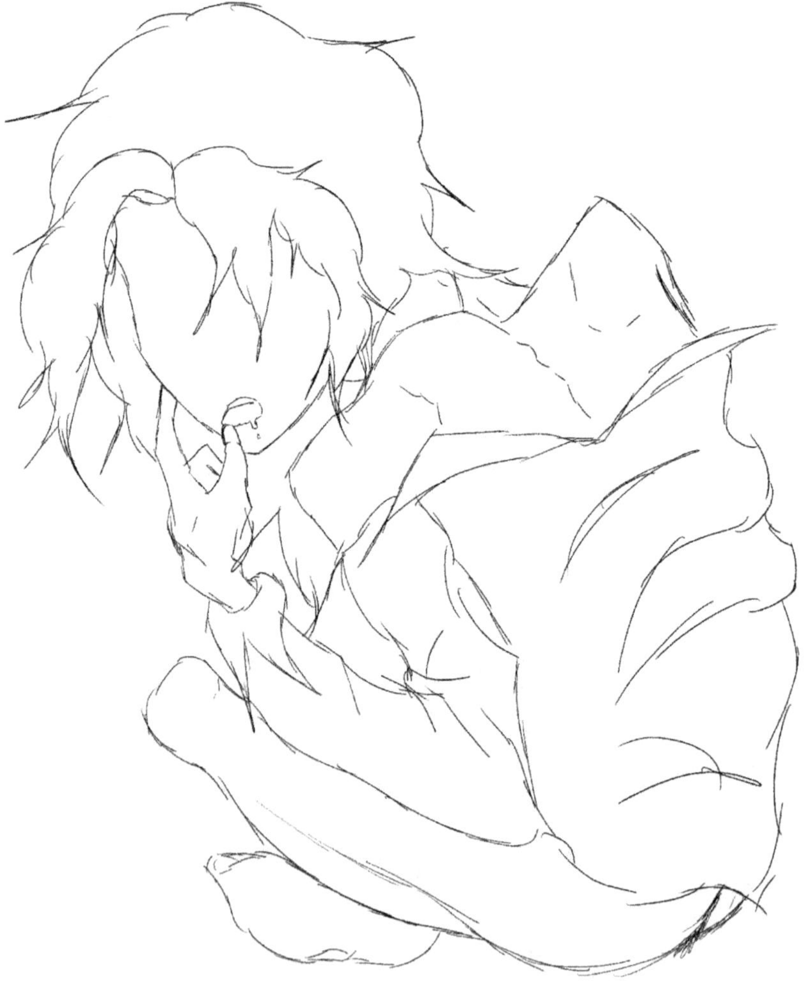

I gained self respect
Like you always asked
Are you upset that now I won't kiss your ass?

I don't believe in happily ever after
If it was real
We'd still be spending our lives together

Just because I show you the broken pieces
Doesn't mean they are ready to be healed

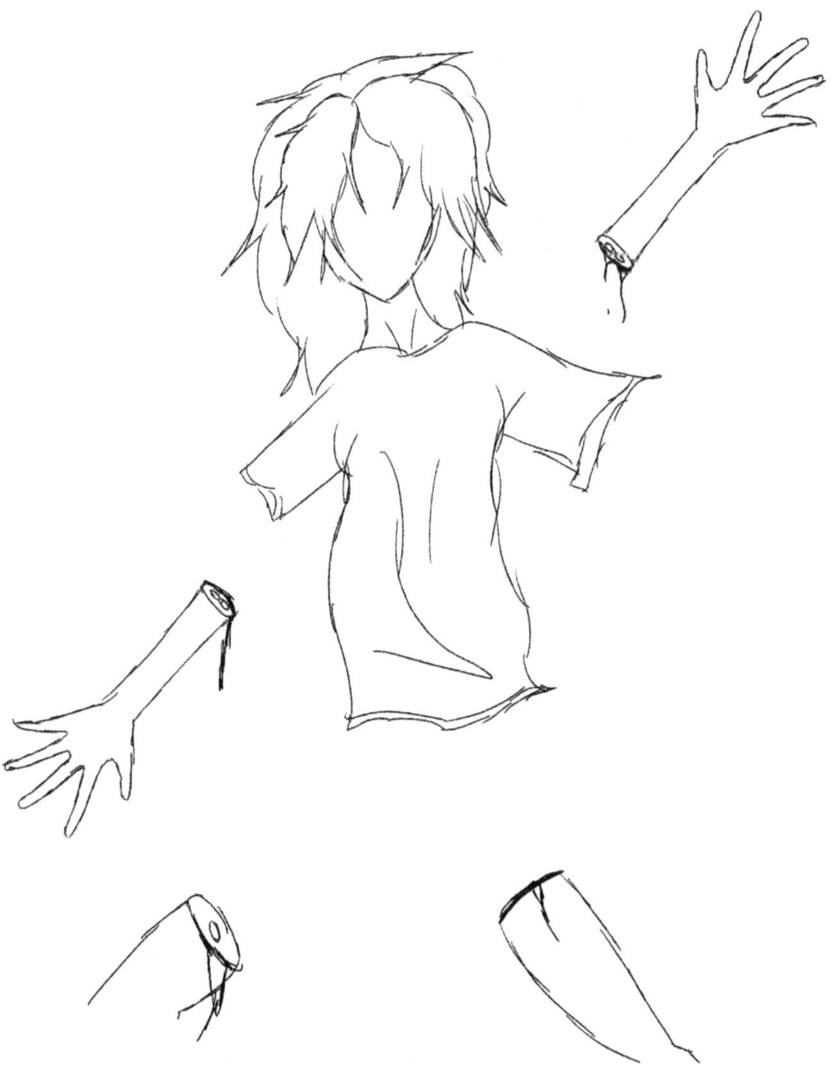

I see you everywhere I go
I think of every memory
And every fantasy of you and me
I wonder if you remember
If I make it
Will you see
Will you be proud of me
Please don't forget
Because I can't stop whispering
Your name under my breath

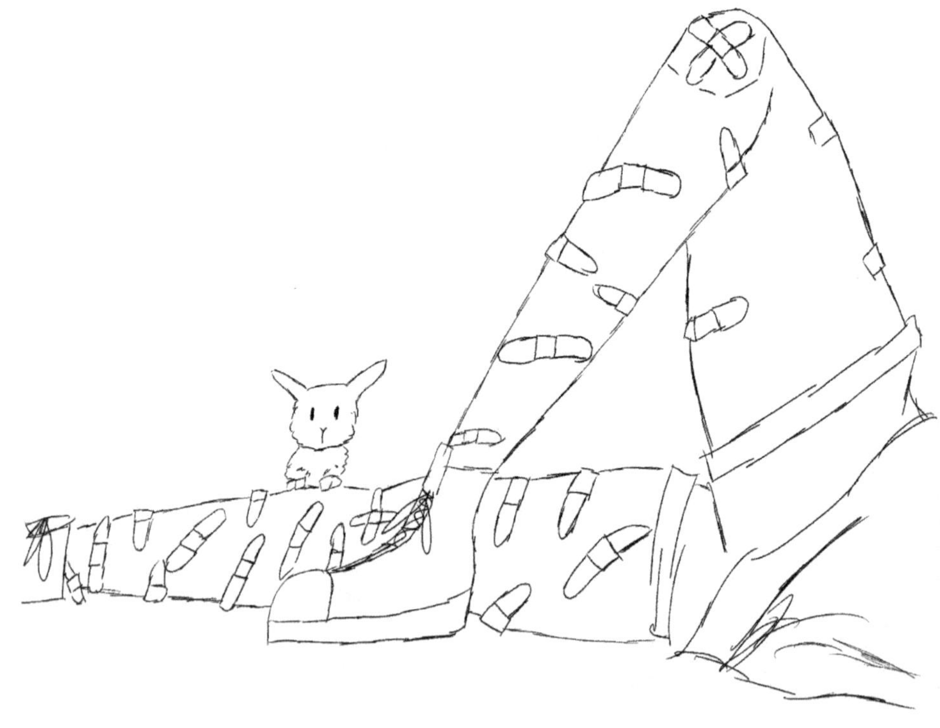

I've lost too many times
To be scared of losing someone
Who only wants me
For the blood they receive
From my lifeless body

You watch me with clouded judgment
Pour poison over my decaying corpse
My rotten mind and weary soul
It is your rains that create something radioactive
Something in my precious garden
That not even you can constrain

Learning how to mold
My definition of my perfect body
To fit the one given to me
Has been one of the most challenging
And exhausting
Acts of love I've done
But its so rewarding
If my fingers are bleeding
And self love is what I'm receiving
My bad days won't define me
My growth is everything
Compared to what I've left behind me

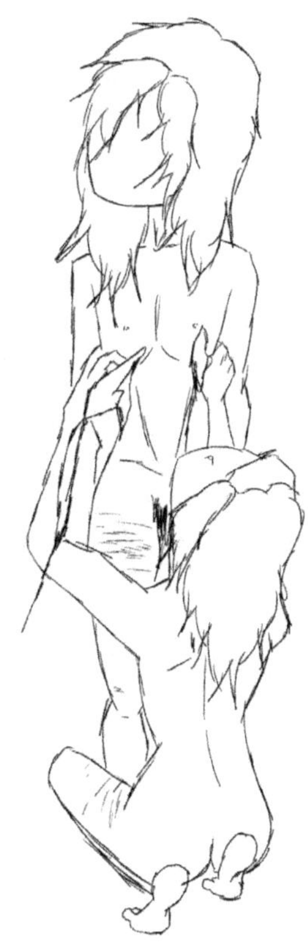

I told you how I felt
You asked me to stop
Because it scared you
Sorry for the emotions I can't control
I'm scared too

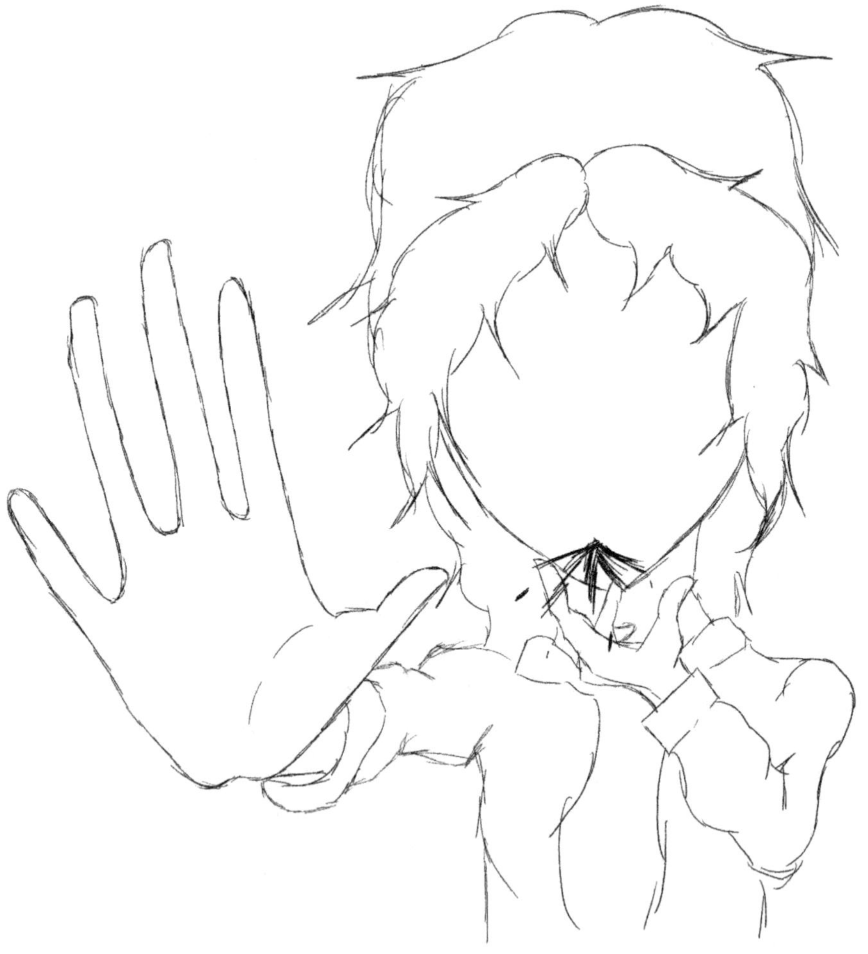

One day I lost everything
I pretended I still had it
And watched the people around me
They knew it was gone
The people who said they'd help me
If I lost my world
Turned their backs on me
Now I realize
It was never them
That gave me the ability to keep going
It was me
And sure they helped
But it was never just them
It was me
And it still is me

You reached out
When I was about to release our friendship
I was done looking at the debris
I didn't know that telling you what you did
Is what I needed in order to be free

How far down can I go?
Will the relief from my aching hands
Be paralyzing when I fall back
And let go of my past?

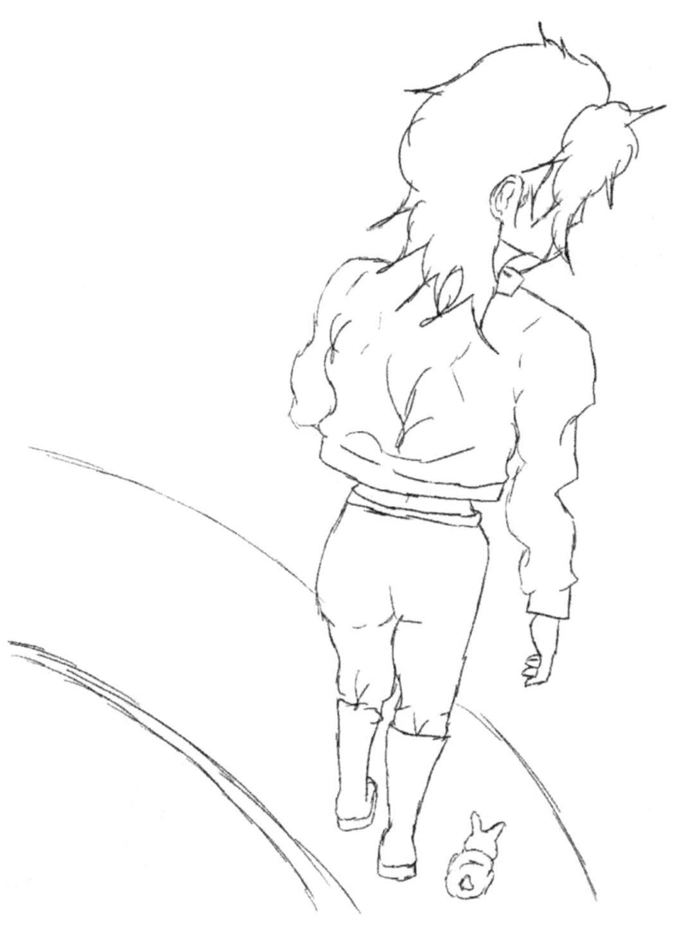

You didn't see what I saw
Never lost what I lost
You didn't have to pay the cost
Weren't dripping with poison from soaking in grief
Like I was
Didn't get stuck in days of disbelief
I have lost my guts
My teeth
My tongue
My lungs
My strength
My bones
I gave away my blood
To people who watched me bruise
What makes you think I'll be scared of losing you?

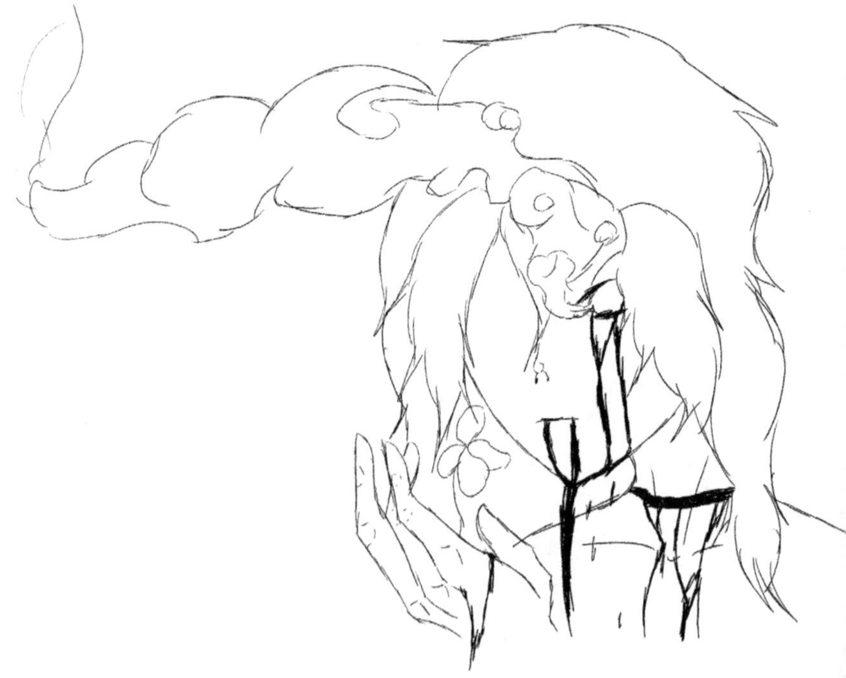

We started out sugary sweet
Now lies about how great you are rot my teeth
Salt looks the same as sugar
But everything is more bitter than before

Never asked you to sacrifice for me
Didn't need your advice.
It would've been nice for you to comfort me
Somehow I'm the root of an issue
Always forced to solve them
I wish to know who I can rely on
Never meant to take from your hand
Learned to lean on them instead
Of having you messing with my head
But I'm still laying in my bed
Wishing I didn't miss you

Do you see all I endure without you
Have you realized I'm impure
Noticed that I was never really sure
I've been acting ever since I learned
I would always be adapting

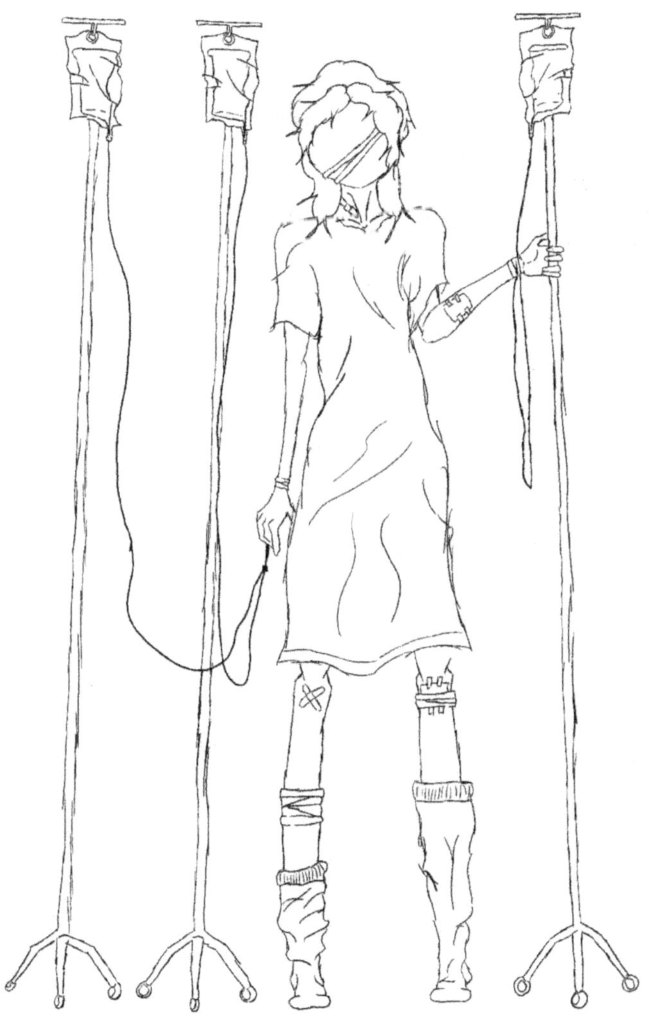

For once I want to drip with power
Instead of leak with pain
This is my wish

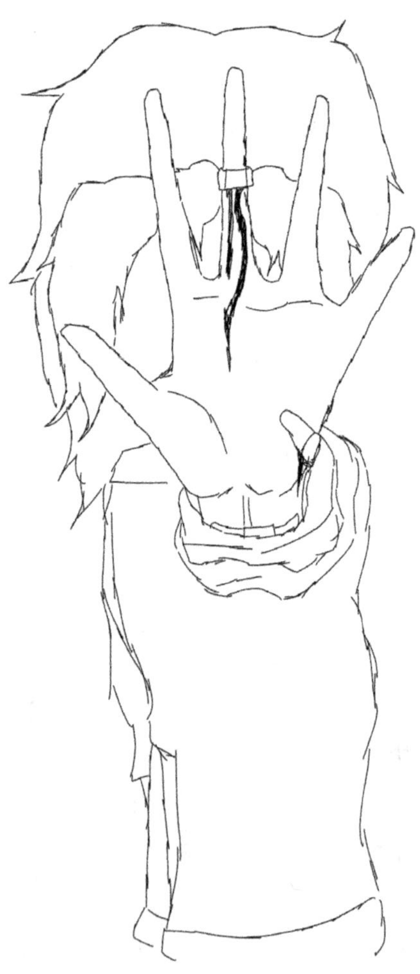

I want to relive every moment with you
To make it feel right
Even if that means dying a thousand more times
I'll forgive everyone but yourself

I am tearing myself apart
Trying to remember what we use to be
I am a suicidal star
You are the weight of my bones
You left me on my own
That's right I was cold
And detached from the earth's soils and stones
Leave me alone
We weren't what I intended for us to be
I wasn't made for you
You weren't made for me

I'm finally starting to get used to this ache and pain
Now you have to hurt me in a new way
Tell me again my ambitions and dreams
Am I forgetting who I wanted to be?
Wake me up from this horrible dream
You call reality

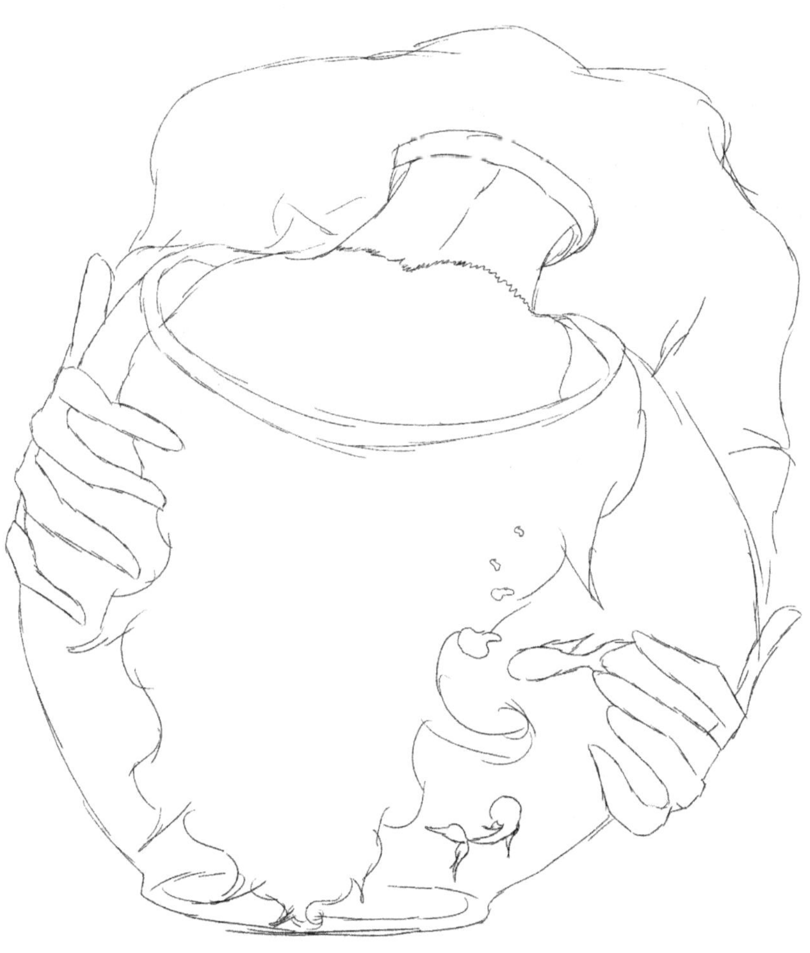

I love and hate
That one of the best summers of my life
Had you in it

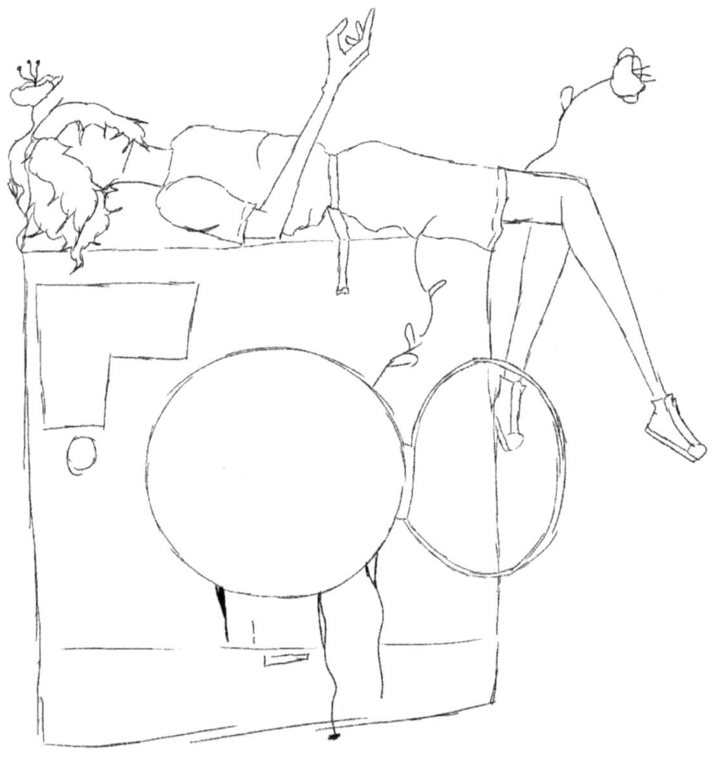

I lay confused
Wishing to scream to you
No sounds come out
What was I thinking about?
I'm losing my mind
Too many questions spiral inside
Not enough time to find all the answers
What is this emotional abuse?
I am used
I am confused

I dropped my past
But couldn't walk away, I didn't want to let go
Even if I had to learn from my mistakes
The choices I've made
I'm tied to the good times those memories
That I don't have to leave behind
Everyone says it's better for me
But I am so used to this discomfort in my own skin
My own mind
I don't care if it'll be my demise
And rot me from inside
It's all I've known
The person who walks alone comforts
And holds their own
They are toxic
Misunderstood
You may never know every piece of them
Because of how much they've left behind
That leaves you with the joy and excitement
Of something mysterious
Society romanticizes it
Everyone wants to see you
Pitied and weak crawling on your knees
To help them feel tall
Do not romanticize what left me traumatized
Hear me scream and understand why I am so bad

No matter how much time we spent
The good and the bad
Will stay in my mind
All the things you said and never did
I was never ready to lose what I lost
It didn't sit right
I still can't rest easy
But once I let go
And it is time
There will be nothing to say
I'm ready to release you
I am sorry to send you away
I hope in my next life our stories will collide
And this time
We do it right

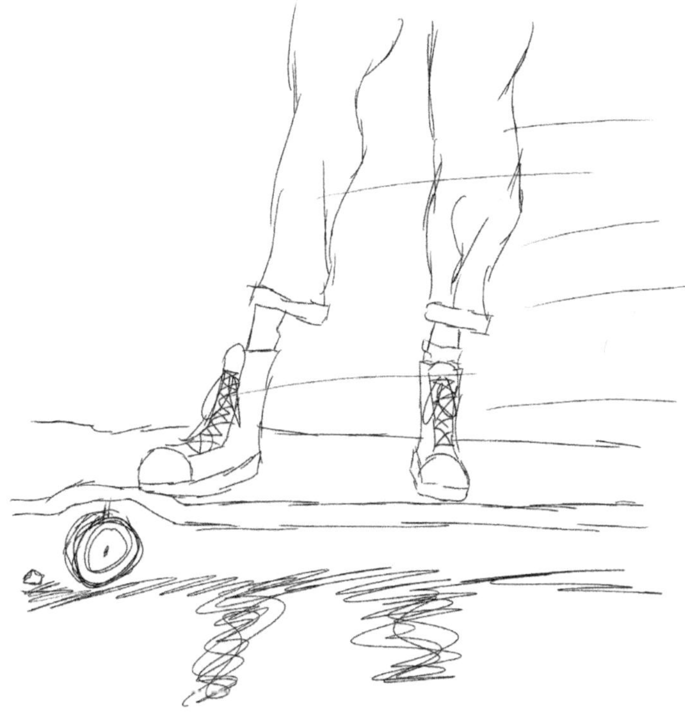

I have something to say
You may not like it
I have no way of putting this sweeter
We are not okay
Our relationship is a violent virus
And I've lost myself in my fever
I'm sick for you
But I can't just wither away
As much as I'd like to
Just to keep you
I have things to do
And lives to change
More things I need to say

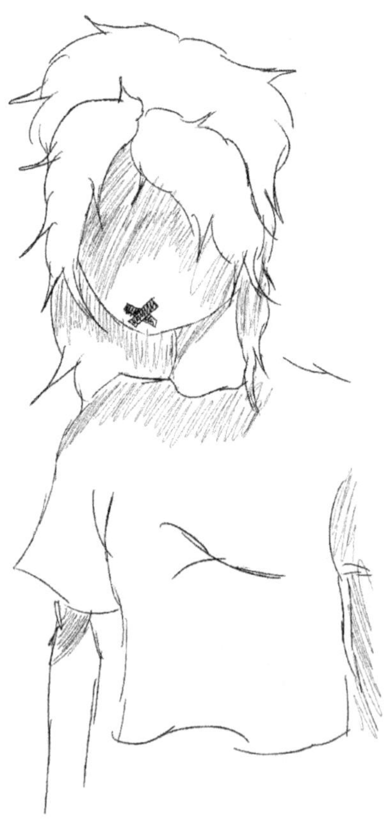

The day the company of my loneliness
Became better than us
Is the day my desire to fuel its fire had risen
You knew that
I've always been driven towards my goals
What made you think I'd hold back for you
What made me actually want to
Vision was too blurred by the good times
So much so I didn't realize the lack of support
I understand if I'm not forgiven
Neither are you
But I had low standards
Just wanted you to be there stand by my side
Didn't have to say a word
It wasn't fair your abandonment
I expected little
Barely anything at all
Just someone to sit with while I fall
Yet with you I was still disappointed

I want you to hurt
I want you to hurt
I want you to hurt so bad
I want you to hurt the way you hurt me
The kind that makes you scream
But choke on your own tears
The kind that forces you to face your fears
By making them reality
I want to make you hurt
I want to hurt you how you hurt me
I want to laugh and tell you
"You're so pathetic"
I want to say I'll be there and then leave
Like you did to me
I want to do to you what you did to me
I want to do it better than you by being worse
Unlike you I'd have to rehearse
I want to but of course
If ever given the opportunity I wouldn't
And if someone did it all for me
If someone hurt you how you hurt me
I'd make sure you were alright
Check in
Every night
I'd help you because I am a fool
I want to stop caring about you
That'll just hurt both of us

Out of sight
Faded away
I never see you these days
But you're never off my mind
Perhaps I'm just blind
-Out of sight Out of mind

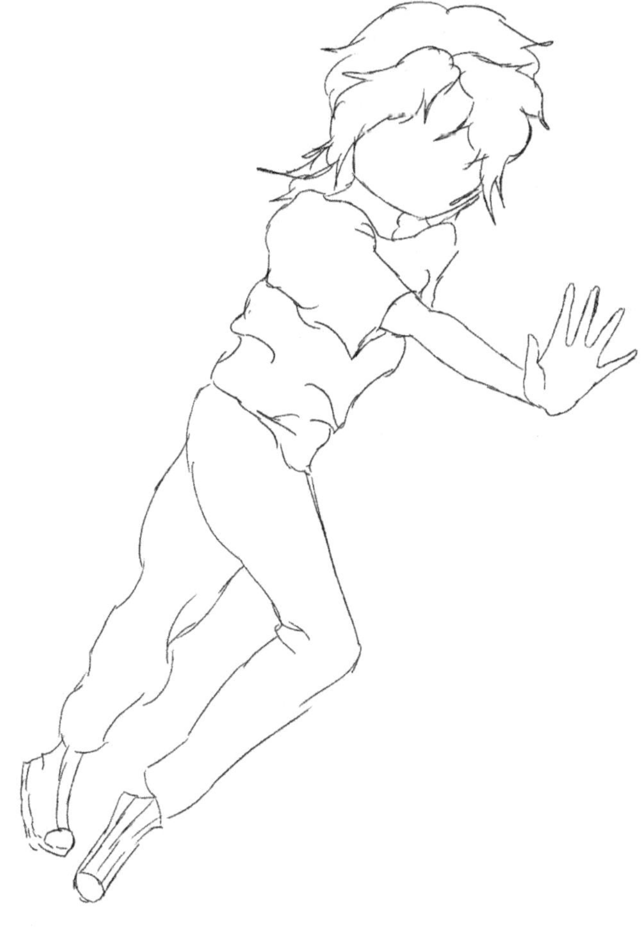

I forget everything
Because I spent so much time in denial
My brain is always on trial
A forgetful suicidal
Who forgot the date of death
To see what was left
But could never take care of themselves
Forgot to eat and shower or brush my teeth
Always falling for my bad habits
My father would constantly yell at me
For never tying my shoes
And for always being in a rush
I finally tied my Timbs together
My boots ready to head off
And they'll give me a boost of speed
Because I no longer had him to catch me
Just myself always
Never anyone else
Because they always say
I'm just being too much
But he'd tell me I'm just more than enough

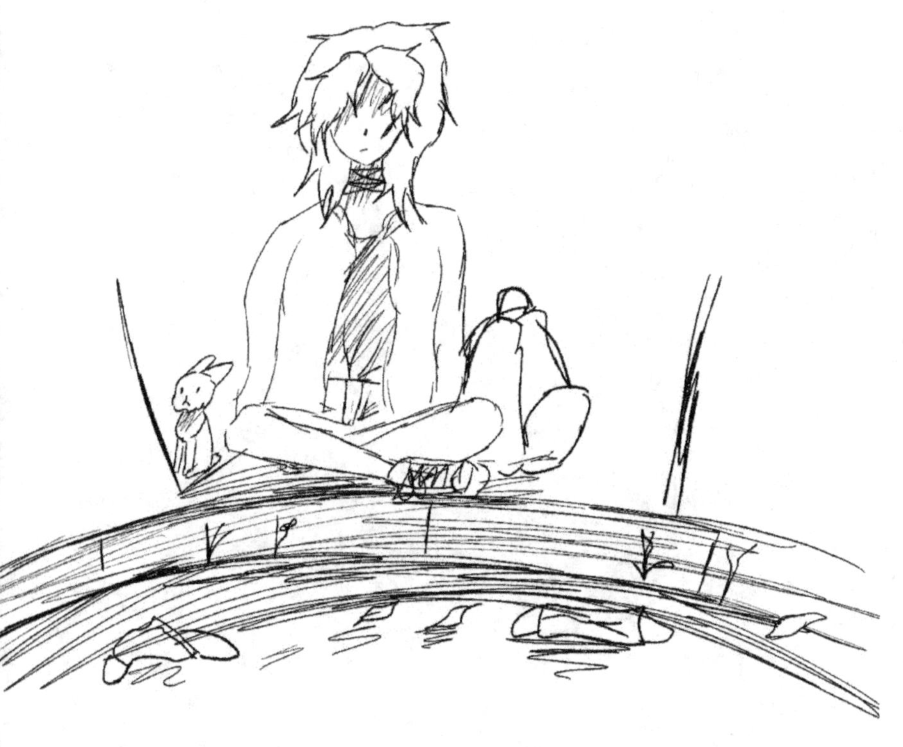

Growing Flowers

You weed a garden before you plant a flower
So why,
Aren't you taking care of yourself
Before helping others?

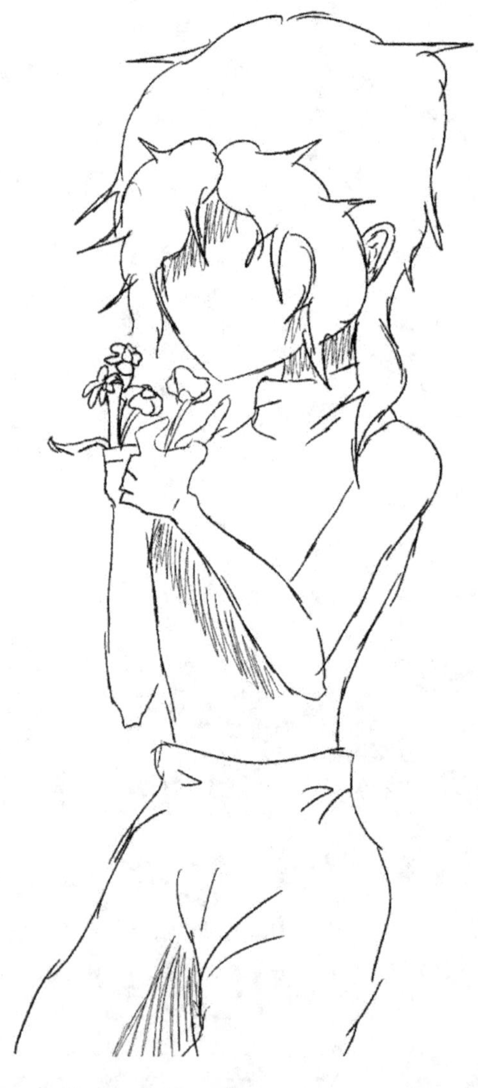

There's always been two sides of me
Both
Nobody wants to see

It's moments like this
The ones where my chest feels full
Of something other than fear
When all the bad things seem to disappear
With you, you make me feel whole
When I don't feel stuck in a state
Of perpetual misery and fear
When I'm thinking of my future
Not the different ways for me to cower
Or reach my grave sooner

My skills were given to me
For me
My skills are used by me
For me
They are merely being shared with you
From me

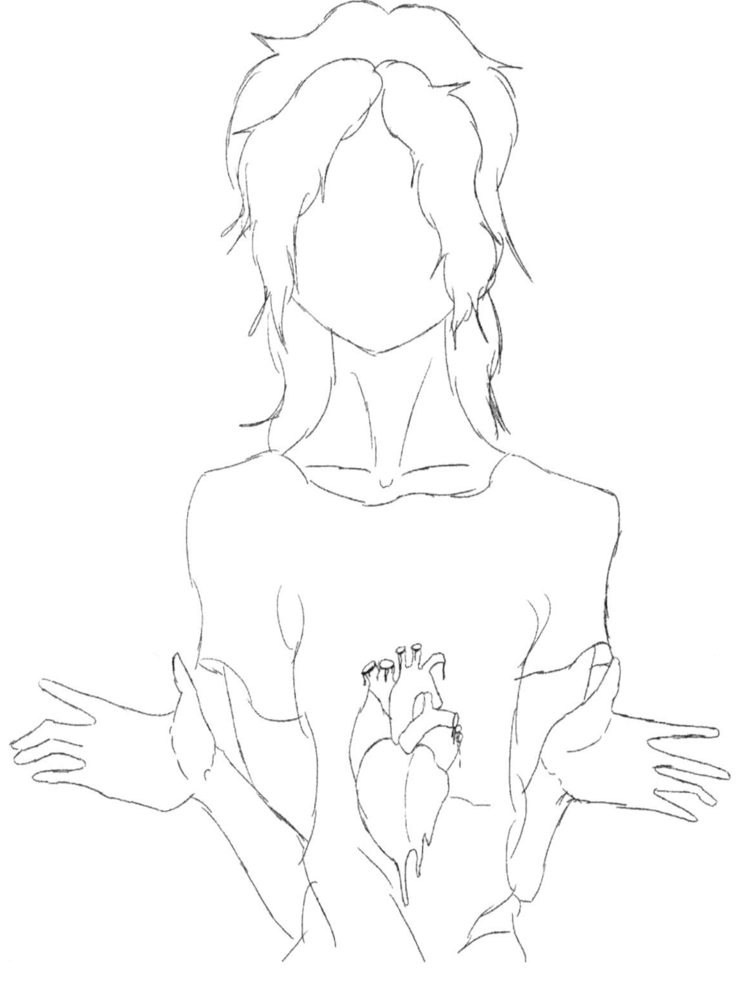

I called it off
Because I knew
That you would just turn me down
Now I'm the one who pushed you around?

I'm not scared of losing anyone anymore
I'm scared of losing my will to become who I want to be

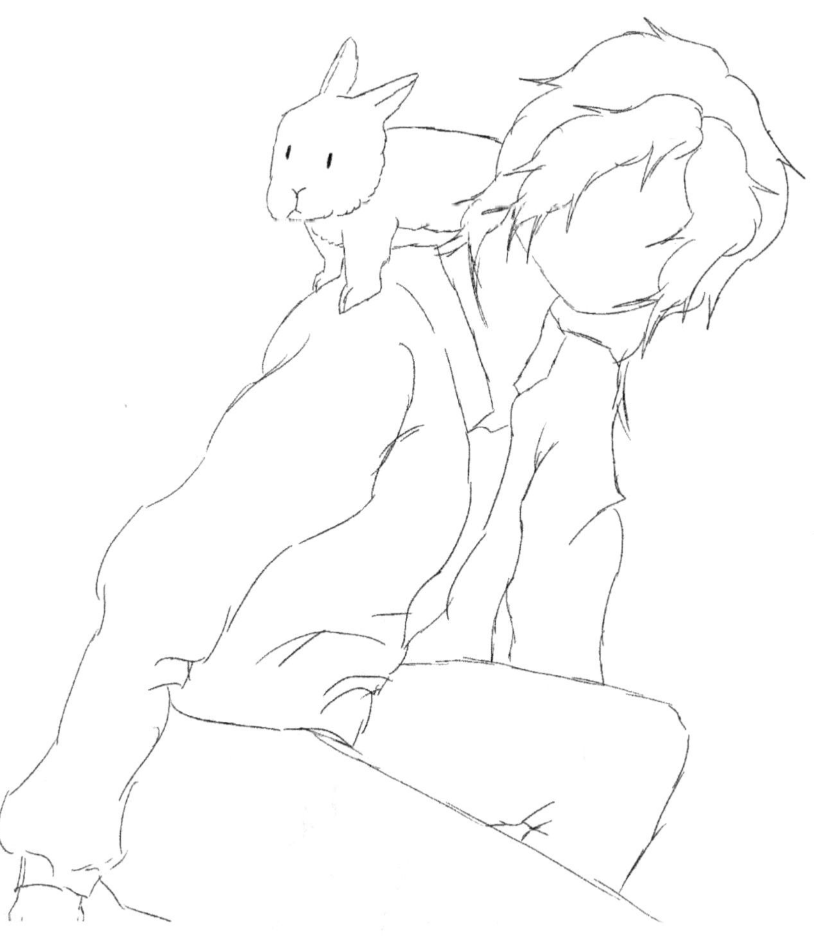

I was there
When you fell apart
I took you into my shelter
Called you a work of art
You said you'd do the same for me
If I fell the way you do
And when I crumbled and fell
You locked yourself away
Leaving me questioning
"Is this all my fault?"
I came to realize
The only fault I played
Was allowing you to rip me inside out

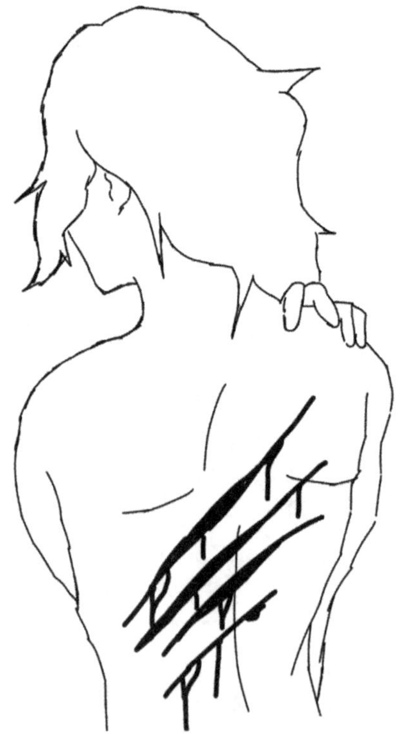

I've lost myself time and time again
Myself, my dreams, and my fears
I lost every ounce of hope I've had
Every reason to smile
To breathe
To merely exist
It left with you
The pain was so much it sparked a flame
And burnt it all to ash
And then those words, they rang in my head
Over and over and over again
I'M SO SORRY
They screamed to you
Now everyone pities me
They try to give me what I please
To make me happy
They know nothing
Will rid your presence from me
I was recently given one of the things
I fantasized about with you
I now know why
It took me so long to admit the truth to myself
Our dreams will be made without you
And it made my chest crumble
It made me hollow
I wish so much to tell you
About what I'm going to do
I will carry on and push through
I will make our dreams come true
My dream, with you

Always so worried about my self expression
I won't tell you about my repression
After my succession

I don't want to be
Your everything
I want to be
The person I see myself as
In my fantasies

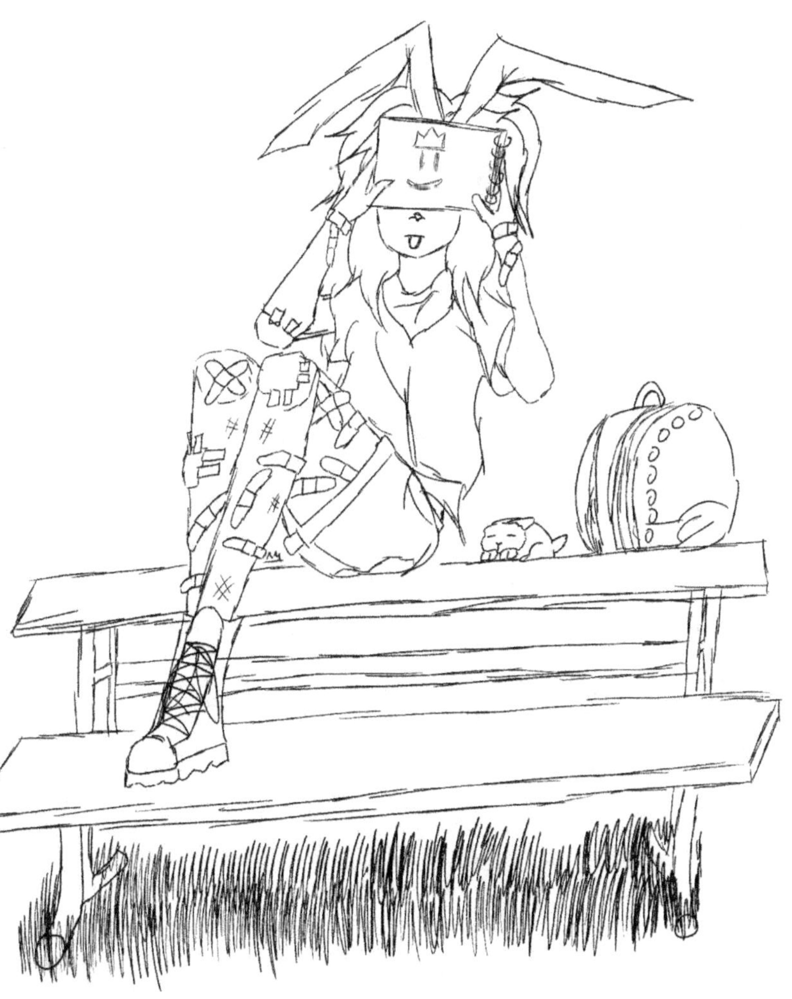

I wouldn't mind if this moment lasts forever
Even if my eyes are tired
I am finally at rest

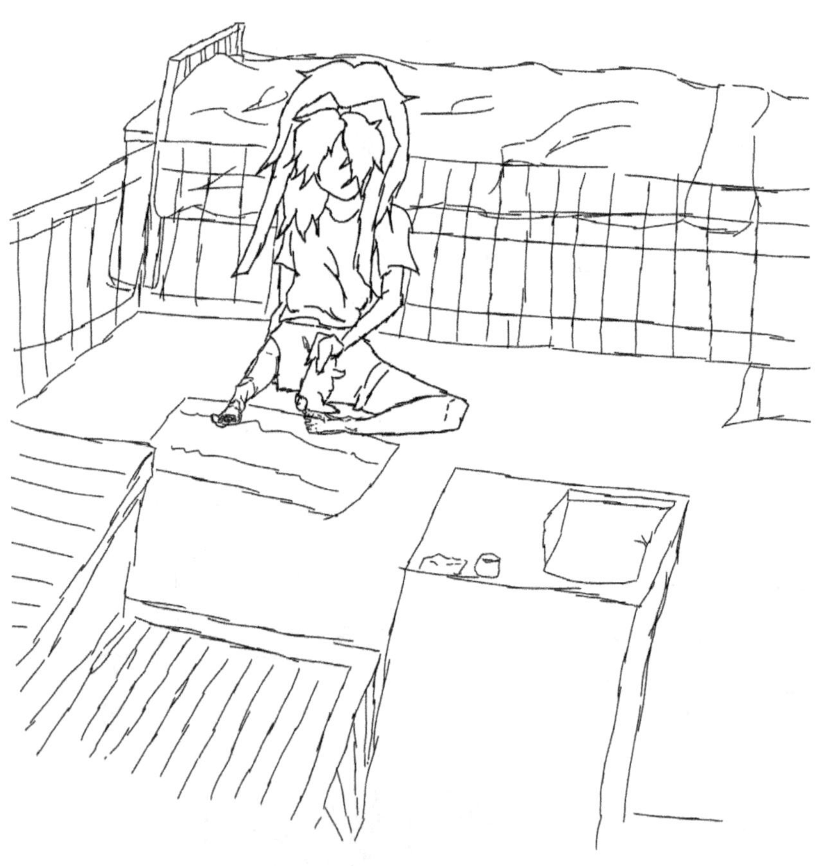

Careful what cards you play
You have no idea what your opponent
Has to say

You left me bleeding and screaming
Lifeless and empty
You sucked out every ounce of me I had
For days I laid drained and accepted my fate
Only for me to realize
I would never fall to the likes
Of someone like you

I thought you were healing me
In a way I guess you did
Because it took losing you
For me to realize how important loving me is

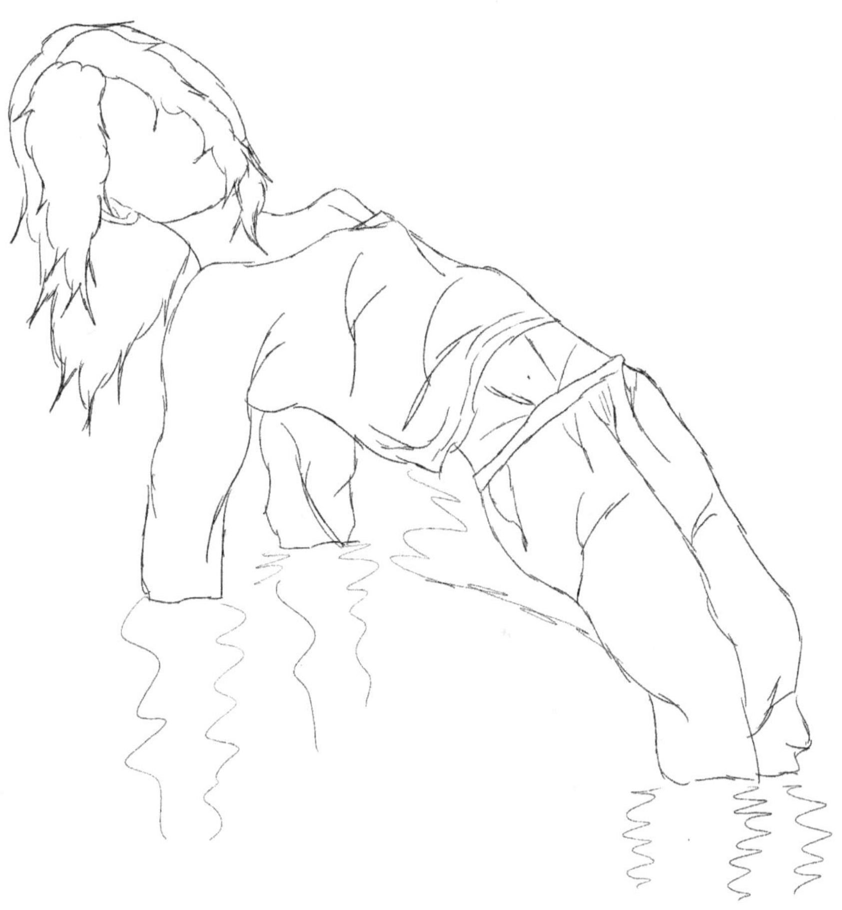

Even those who are silent are dangerous
They are watching your every move
And learning every way to destroy you

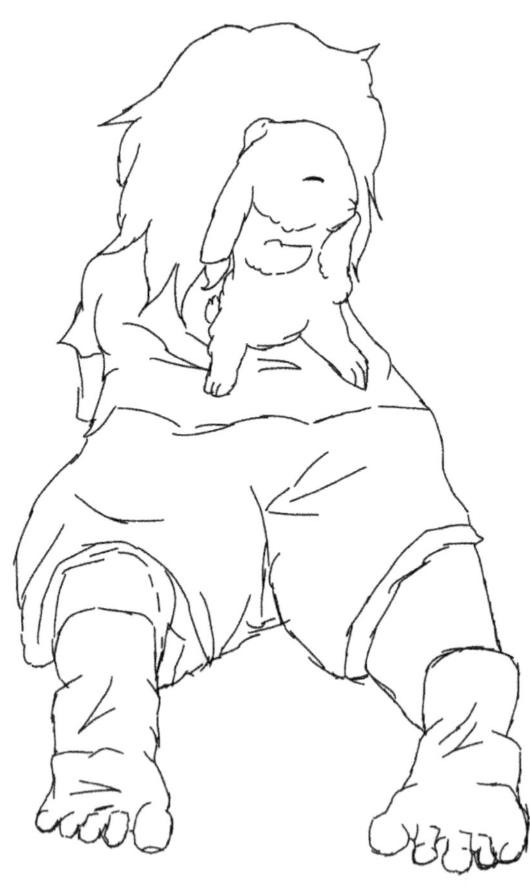

Just because I got set back
Doesn't mean I'll hold back
I've got less to lose
And more to risk

When I was younger
I told people my favorite flower was a dandelion
To which people would answer
"It's a weed"
But it seemed to me that this weed was a flower
Attempting to spread hope
I could mask it into a wish
A thousand wishes if I searched long enough
They were never hard to find
Just waiting for me to see
I used every seed on the same dream

I'll rearrange the words and letters
Turn them into something
I like the sound of

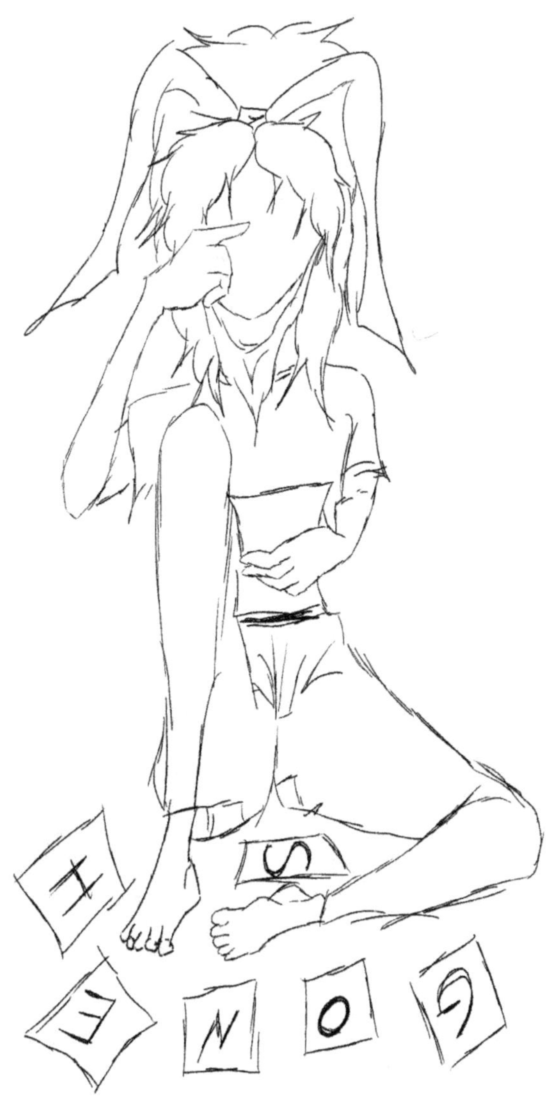

I’ve lived many lives
I can tell you about each one
Explain and complain
About how I’ve died
What made me revive
Why I didn’t survive
Each life was a little different from the others
I wasn’t meant to be in any
There were already many
I was plenty
Each life I regret not speaking my mind
If I had I would’ve just thrived

My fantasies wilted like a dying flower in my palms
The thorns scraped open my skin
I bleed a bright crimson red
I saw it's beauty but felt it's consequences
And regardless of what others felt for me
I cared for them the way I felt necessary
And new opportunities spread

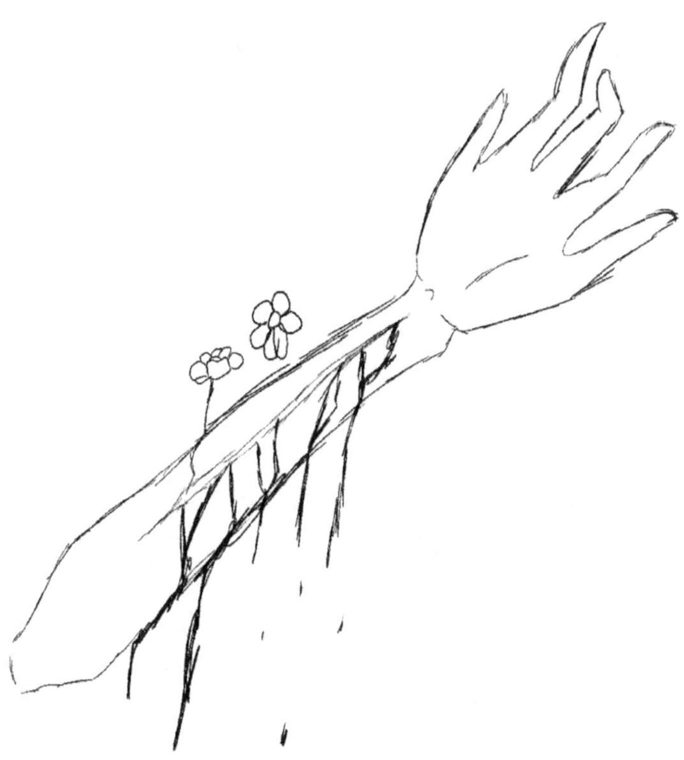

I don't expect you to read my mind
Or understand why I'm lying all the time
Don't expect you to lend a hand or take a stand
Just want you to pretend you want me to make it
So when I wake
I don't have to befriend the scary thoughts
I meet

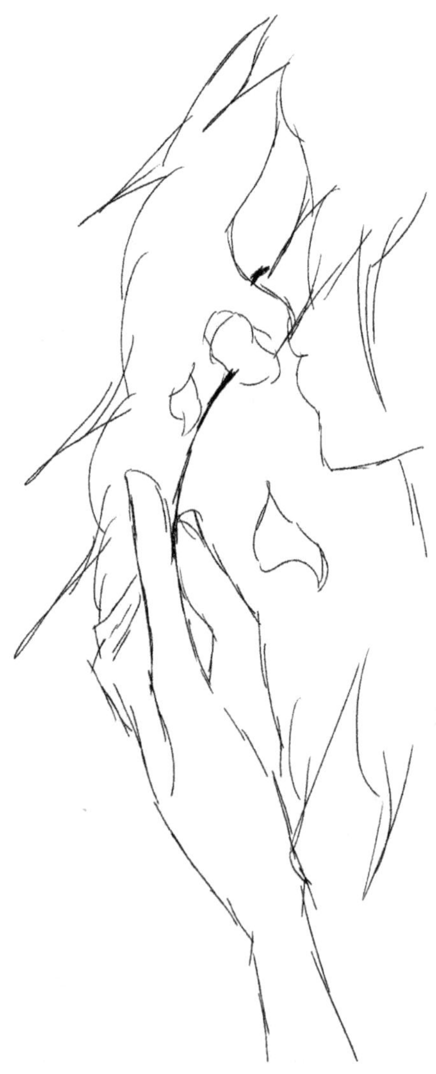

I've always wanted
My art to form a place in someone's heart
Start a thought in their mind
To touch their soul
In a palace they weren't aware of
Make them rewind
My words ringing in their head
My illustrations dancing to the pouring chimes
Making them remember both good and bad times
"Write the book"
My ambitions would remind
One day I would finally decide
To vomit every word coming to my mind

I'm blood stained and scarred
My skin is a destroyed work of art
This body has felt pain
That only makes up a small portion of my brain
But who am I to complain about all I've lost
It was the cost of my name
I don't want fame
Just want to feel okay
About the emotions flowing through my veins
I am only a reminder that those who climb
Are the ones that get higher

I'm an artist
I take in every moment
Choke on the creativity that fills my chest
I am obsessed with trying my hardest
Do not be alarmed by this
What helps me breathe will always kill me slowly

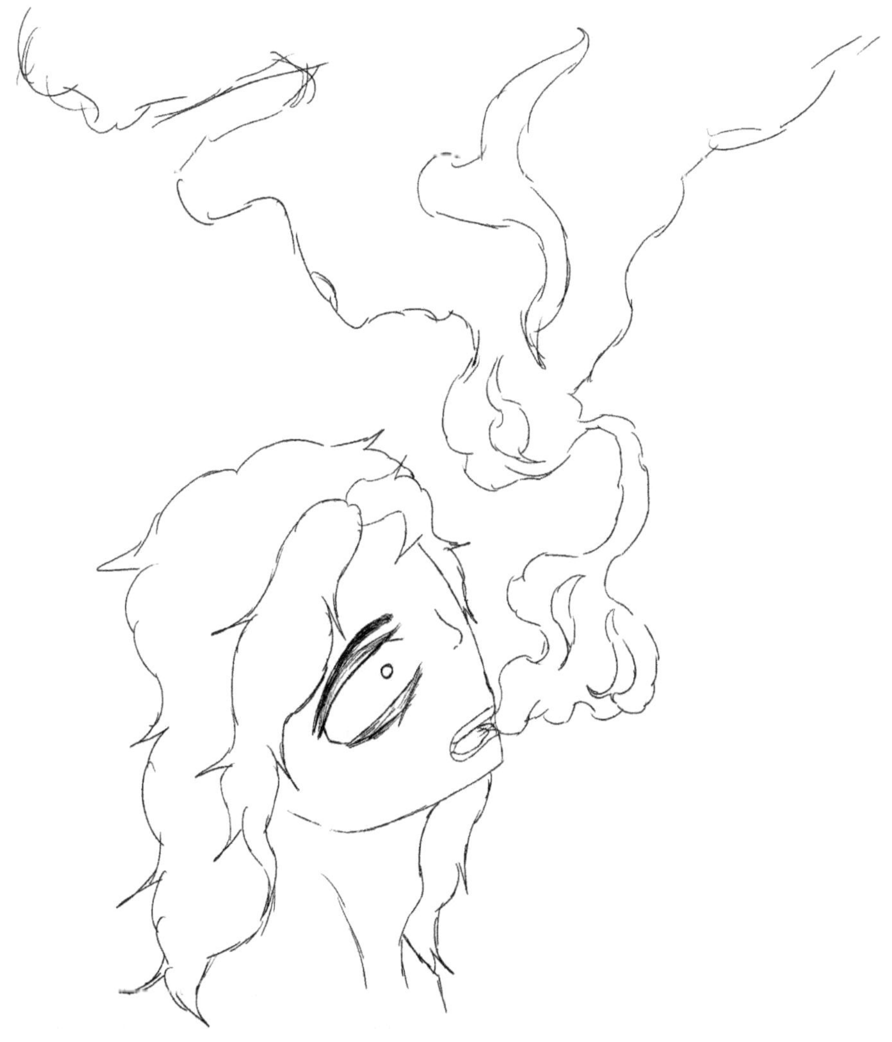

What did it feel like
Watching me slip out of your control
Fade away
For me it felt great
To have relief from your pain

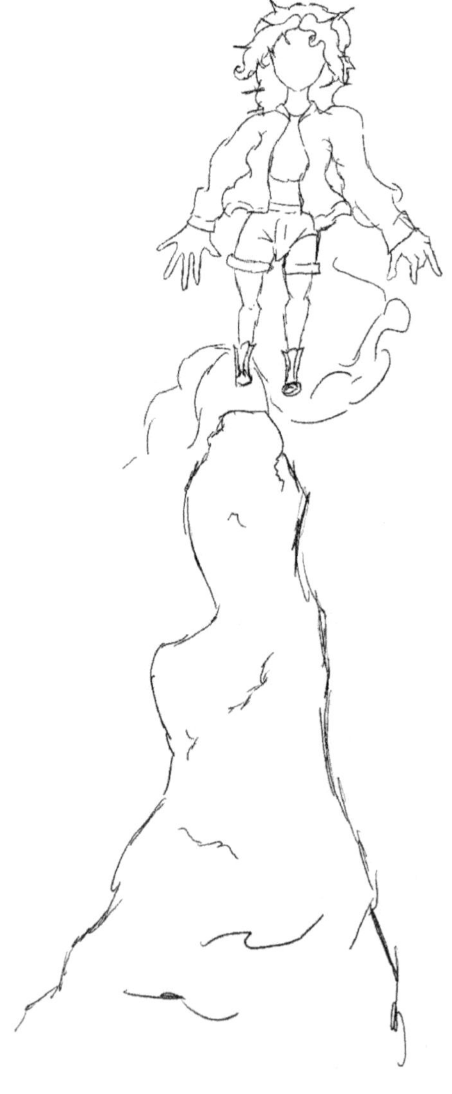

This isn't my first time dying
So stop your crying
I'll come back and keep trying
This is the curse of always reviving

You're losing all the different parts of me
Are you petrified
What do you prefer
For me to remain a blur
Everyone wanted this
Everyone wants to gather like a circus
Let me entertain you
Your satisfaction is worthless
Let me undo what I've been taught
No longer containing and straining
Now releasing for your pleasing
Just like always
You're the only one that sees change
I've been blindfolded
Hiding in the dark
Did this go too far
Ashes come out summoned from my safe place
To open my heart
Now you tear me apart
It's judgment on my art my life my thoughts
Everything I do
You murder me and beg me to stay promising
We'll be okay

There are no heroes or villains
Here
There are people
We are trying

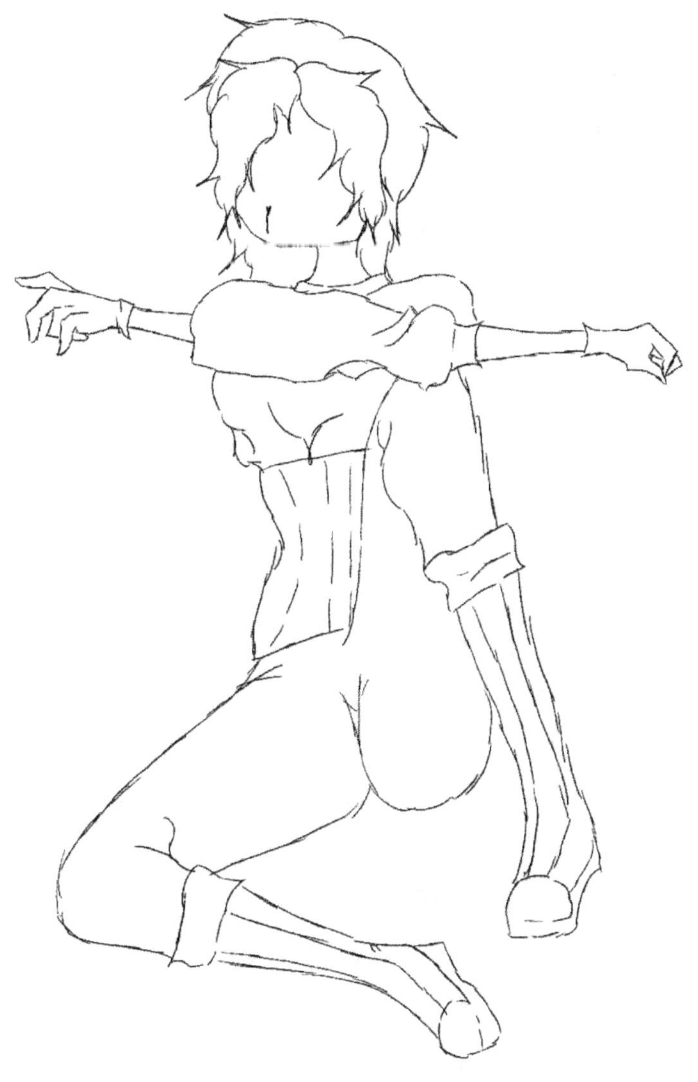

I started a new life
One that would be better for me
But now I see
How hard healing can be
I found myself screaming in excruciating pain
I forgot my name
Not looking for fame
Just to teach people that I'm the same
Equivalent
But I can never seem to let go
Of what hurts the most

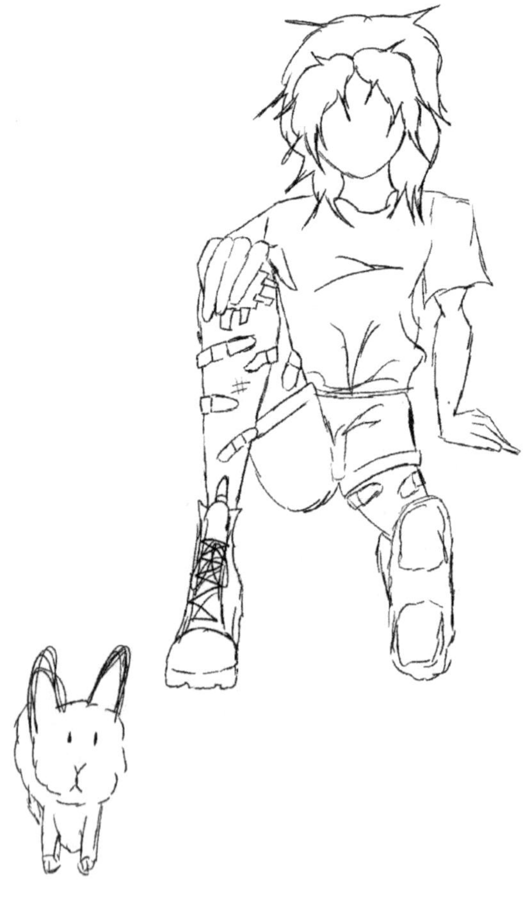

Time moves differently for me
Six months ago was yesterday
I still feel the fresh wounds
Even though I'm picking at the scab
And this morning was a decade ago
I am fighting my mind
To remember when I got up today

My anxious thoughts intrude
The process of healing
It's not what they claimed it would be
So many ups and downs
Just trying to fix me
Let me explain the battle I face everyday
It's like remembering I left my stove on
But instead of it being as easy
So easy
At the flick of the switch so it stays off
The fire remains on
I fight it and once it goes out
They burn again brighter and bigger than before
They beacon me to join them one last time
Promising safety and comfort
This constant battle with my own burnt ashes
I knew I was always fascinated by this fire
The one that burned my bones
And anything that would destroy my frame
But build my name
Making me my own king

I told myself to not miss what we had
There was no point in turning back
But the memories of the good times
They flood my brain
As glad as I am that we had our times
Take your memories
They are no longer any good to me
Even the healthy ones hurt me

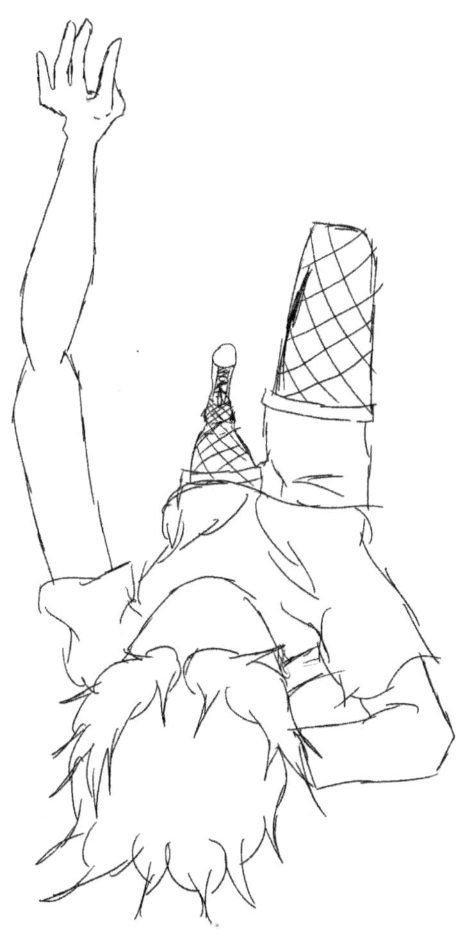

My mind's image is violent
So I remained silent
Didn't mean to startle you
I'm bleeding
That's not what I meant to do
You keep pleading me to stop
They're just intrusive thoughts
So careless and reckless
Let's settle this
Because they become
More common when I'm overwhelmed
Could you please slow down
So I don't have to yell and pour out

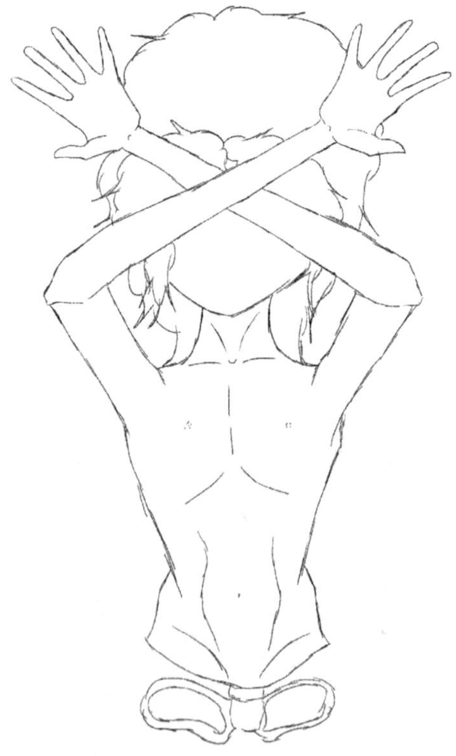

I hyper-fixate
I'm too obsessive
My thoughts and action repeat
I rot from this disease that I've become
We are one
It's so bad so unhealthy
But it feels so good it seems so right
Who am I without these toxic traits
I want to make some major mistake
That ends with my blood and a white face
When did all these thoughts take place
These emotions have resurfaced
I can't seem to remember my purpose
It's getting bad again
Part of me doesn't want it to end
Can't tell anyone I don't want past progress
Just current destruction
This environment is so problematic
My nerves are ecstatic
I'm alive and dead
Rotten in my bed
Unable to leave my head
I'm the problem
I'm ill with no medicine
It is what I'm capable of in this sickness
That I dread

I am littered with my own impurities
Trashed with insecurities
These adjectives could never define me
I'm an artist and poet
Who's always at a loss of what they see in themselves
But I see great significance
I can perfectly describe something else
Living so deeply in every moment
My mind drifts away
Never truly wanted to stay
Just want to see what's possible
If I can really be unstoppable
If others can relate
Or if I could say what they feel and think
Like my idols did for me
Weird to think that once
I got the idea there was a possibility
I could become like them
The minute my pen hit the paper I was
The only difference is I am so insignificant
In the cloud of judgment
The only expectations I have to fulfill are my own
And I am never someone I can condone

They said that time heals
How long until I forget
How excruciating this pain feels
Time hasn't healed me
It's given me more to achieve
More to stay silent and cry about
More things to say that you'll never see me receive
For them to pout complain
That they believed you'd be proud
Are you even listening
Because I can't hear a sound

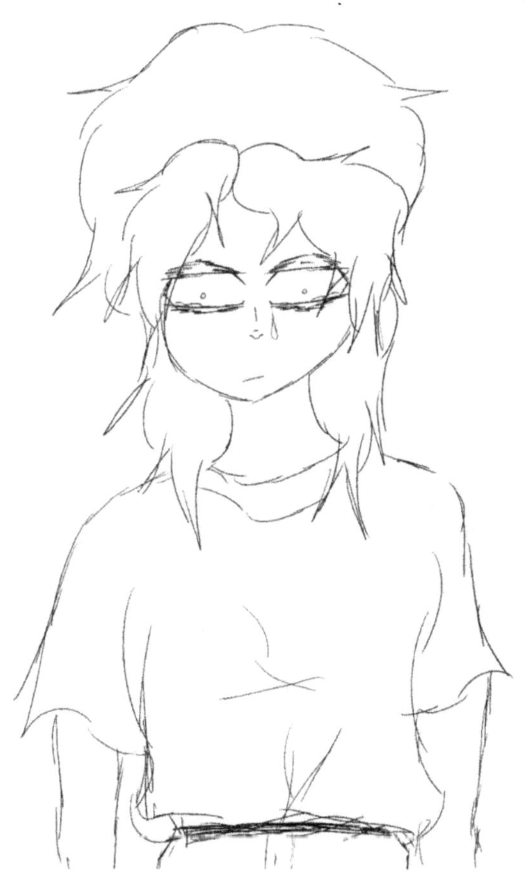

Is this even mine
I'm just floating above
Watching it all
Feeling physical pain but no emotion
No love
Swaying through the motions like a tire swing
I'm being swung my reality is distorted
Pulled down by gravity
I try to stand from my knees
Vision is too blurry to see
Heads too dizzy to focus
I'm not connected. I can't control this body
Can't get it to walk right
This vessel isn't me

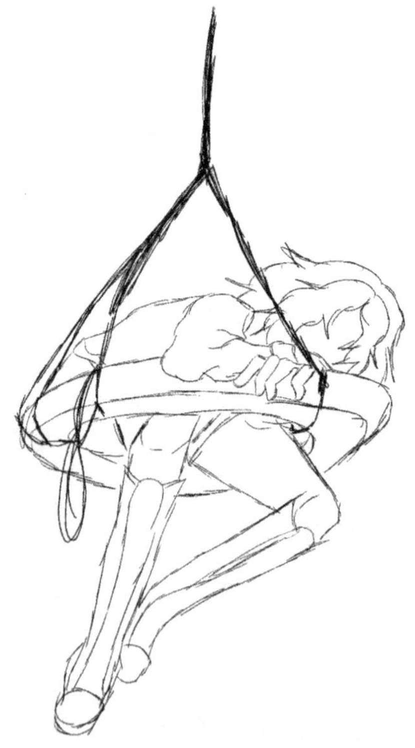

I'm part of something greater than myself
But the truth of my insignificance
Rains down like hell
Everything I do is a waste
Everything about me will be left
Forgotten in this place

I truly believe in order to know what is good
You need bad
And if this is some lie
It is one I am okay living by
It makes it easier for me to get to know myself
Less hard to ask for help
I cannot deny this damage that's been done
The harm that has been inflicted
I've become addicted
It can happen to anyone

If I knew it would hurt that bad
I wouldn't have done it
Now that I know what I've made myself from it
I'd do it again

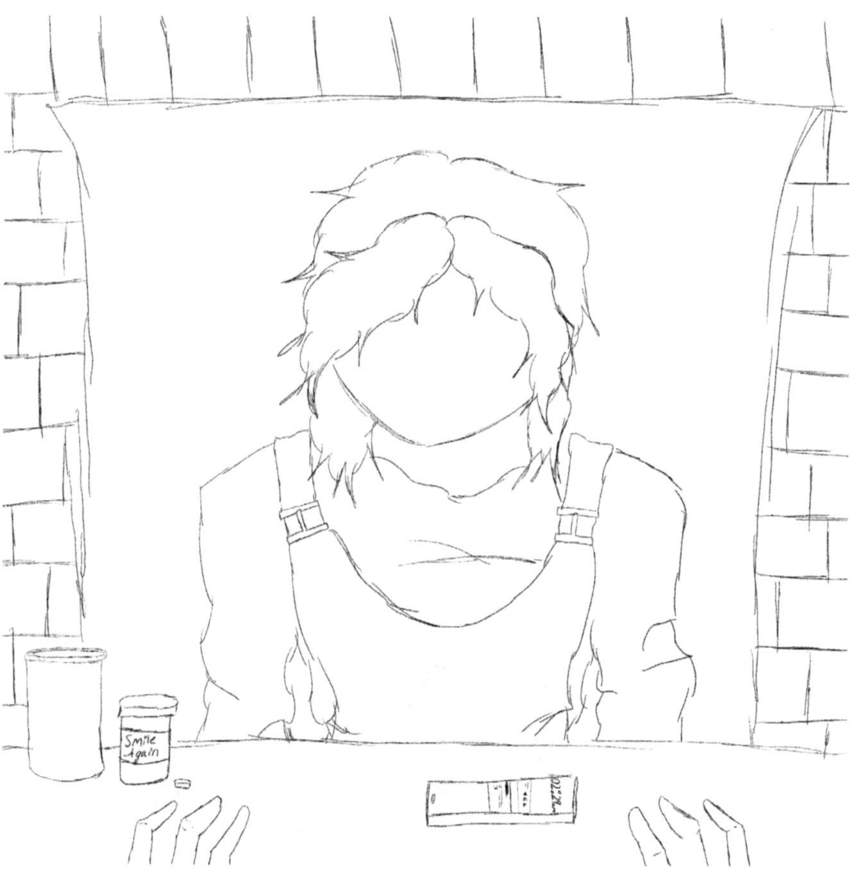

I was the dough
My mirror the cookie cutter
The numbers the blade that made
Cookies shaped like stars
I counted them as calories

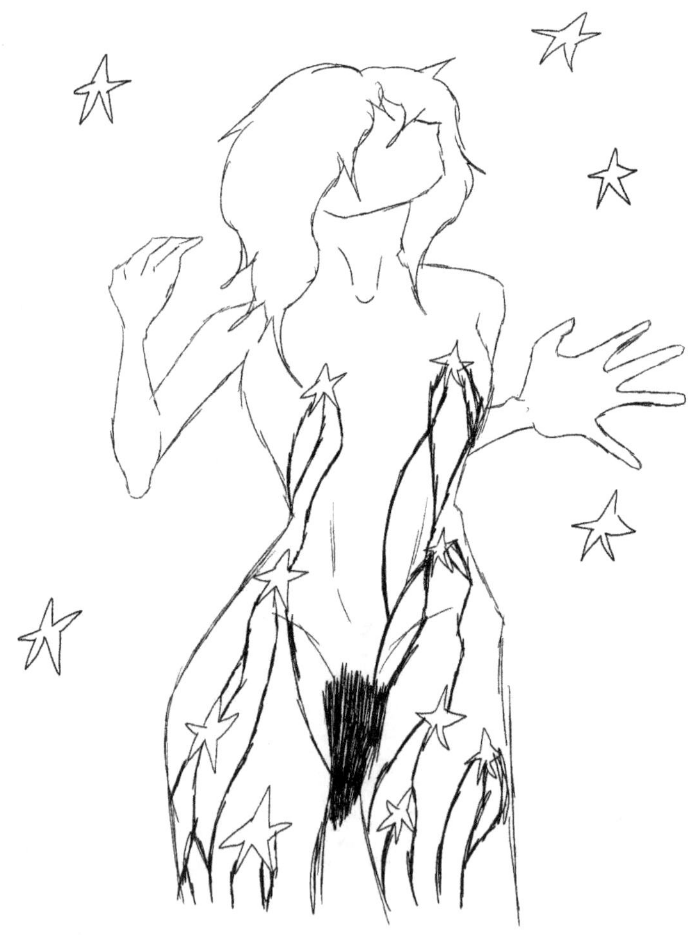

No one will remember me
Or my work
We're all going to die
You reading this may not remember it
It may not reside in your mind
This is worthless
You'll leave it all behind
Nothing I do matters
But at the same time
I might change one life
One thought
Dammit I have to do this because
Time is endless
And I am pointless

To everyone with tired eyes
Sad lullabies
With glass hearts and silver scars
From tearing themselves apart
That hide under baggy clothes
Their thighs, wrists shoulders and stomachs
That cover up with that easy white lie, the little
I'm *fine*
It's OK to cry
I'll listen to you weep
Wipe your tears from your cheek
And I'll hold you until you finally sleep

You are everything you put your mind to

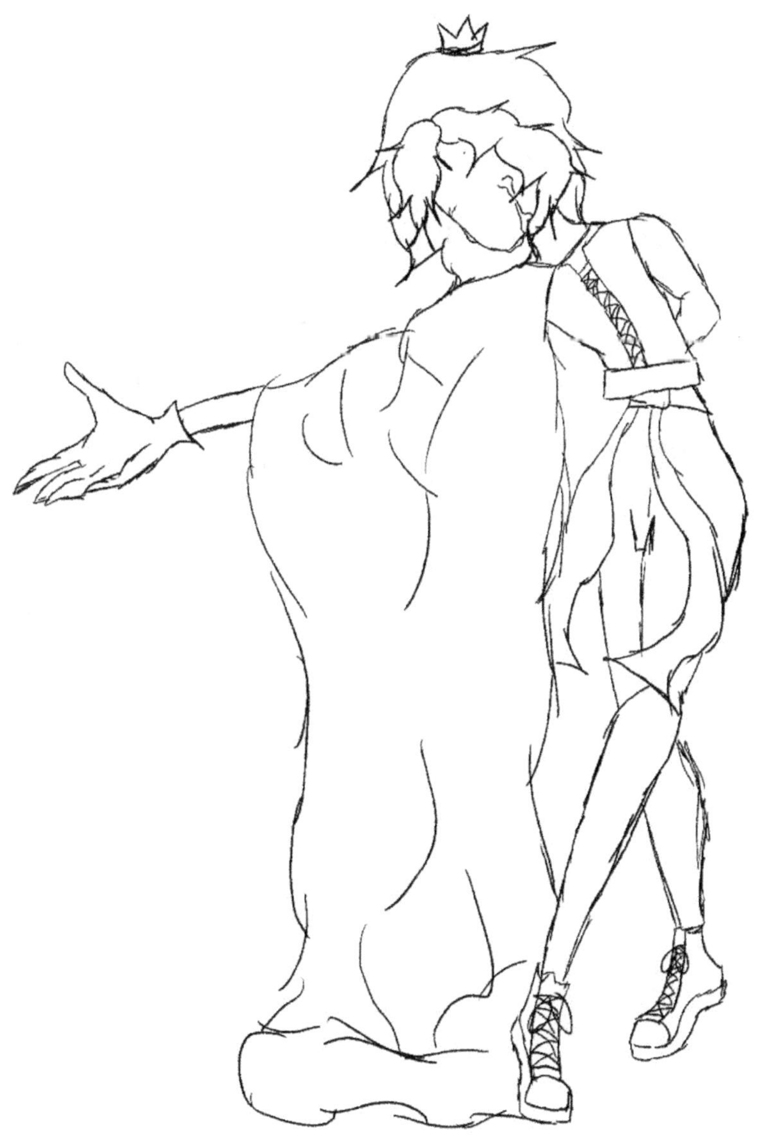

The process of making this book has been so hard but so rewarding. It may not seem hard, throw a few scribbles and notes into a document then transfer it to a file, sure, piece of cake. Every poem in here; every word, every sentence, every drawing. Every emotion, the pain, the confidence, the resentment, I have felt. I have gone through it all in order to bring this to you. It means a lot, you mean a lot. You matter, you are everything you set your mind to.

Your story doesn't end here ;

Always yours, Royal.

Royal is a digital artist, and now a poet.
They've written and formatted this book on their own. They also drew all the pictures. There will be more books in the future. If you really liked this, don't just look here, you can also check on Instagram!
Instagram: @freakish_illustrations

www.ingramcontent.com/pod-product-compliance
Lightning Source LLC
LaVergne TN
LVHW010613100826
845148LV00014B/2948

* 9 7 9 8 2 1 8 2 1 7 3 6 5 *